The Lobster Gangs
of Maine

The Lobster Gangs
of Maine

James M. Acheson

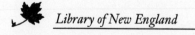

Library of New England

University Press of New England
Hanover and London

UNIVERSITY PRESS OF NEW ENGLAND
publishes books under its own imprint and is the publisher
for Brandeis University Press, Dartmouth College, Middlebury
College Press, University of New Hampshire, Tufts University,
and Wesleyan University Press.

University Press of New England, Hanover, NH 03755
© 1988 by University Press of New England
Printed in the United States of America   10   9   8   7   6   5

Library of Congress Cataloging in Publication Data

Acheson, James H.
  The lobster gangs of Maine.

  Bibliography: p.
  Includes index.
  1. Lobster fishers—Maine.   2. Lobster fisheries—
Maine.   I. Title.
HD8039.F66U473   1988   338.3'7253841'09741   87–40506
ISBN 0–87451–437–1
ISBN 0–87451–451–7 (pbk.)

Dedication

To Helen, Julie, Jim, Marion, Liz, Katie, and Daniel

Contents

Illustrations

Preface

This book evolved from several different field projects that spanned fifteen years and had different sponsors and aims. In 1970 I was a research associate on a University of Maine manpower research project (U.S. Department of Labor). From fall 1972 to spring 1974 I worked on a National Marine Fisheries Service Project concerned with fisheries management. During these periods, I did my initial work on the territorial system, the social structure of harbor gangs, fishing skill, and attitudes toward various management proposals. For some time I led a double existence, teaching during the week and commuting to the coast on weekends to interview lobstermen and measure lobsters.

From 1974 to 1975 I worked for the National Marine Fisheries Service (Fisheries Management Branch) in Washington, D.C. During this time, I visited Maine for only a week in January to observe the entire lobster fleet turn to shrimping.

In the spring of 1977, the University of Maine Sea Grant Office funded my research on the social structure of three communities along the central Maine coast. That summer, I studied the diffusion of wire lobster traps in central Maine.

My most important fieldwork was done from September 1977 to 1980, when I was principal investigator for a large-scale project with an equally large title—"University of Rhode Island/University of Maine Study of Social and Cultural Aspects of Fisheries Management in New England under Extended Jurisdiction"—sponsored by the National Science Foundation (grant number AER 77-06018). The purpose of this project was to gather data for analysis of the newly passed Fisheries Management and Conservation Act (PL 94-265). I obtained much of the data presented here at that time.

This project had two crews, one operating out of the University of Rhode Island under supervision of Dr. John Poggie, the other from the University of Maine under my direction. In the fall of 1977, we studied the three communities that yielded our information on kinship and social structure of Maine fishing towns. From March to December 1978, we compiled a profile of every harbor in New England, studying also the diffusion of innovations and attitudes toward resource management. In Maine, we focused on similarities and differences among the three largest fisheries (lobster, groundfish, and herring). For this project, our crews rode lobster boats to collect quantitative data on the factors influencing catches. We measured more than ten thousand lobsters. This so-called Carapace Measuring Project provided a good deal of information on skills and other factors influencing catches, which are reported in some detail in chapter 5. In this study, we interviewed many skilled fishermen and four lobster biologists about the factors influencing catches.

In 1984, I interviewed extensively on the marketing system and in 1986, on changes in attitudes toward management. Data from all these investigations have been useful in development of this book.

Material for this book comes from all the communities along the central Maine coast from Bailey Island in the west to Brooksville. Although more of the information came from the harbors of Bristol than from any other single community, this volume cannot by any means be considered a community study. Indeed, the objectives of this book could not have been attained through just one community, since men from one harbor compete for fishing area with men from several others. Moreover, the networks that influence everything from marketing to the spread of innovations extend beyond the boundaries of any single community.

The present volume is a highly condensed version of the original manuscript of some seven hundred pages. For academics in my own field of social anthropology and in related fields of study, the documentation exists in a dozen or more of my own articles and reports, which are listed in the bibliography. These studies and other primary and secondary sources cited would be superfluous for many readers but are available for the scholar or the specialist.

My education as a social anthropologist at the University of Rochester helped me to look at my own state—Maine—as any anthropologist looks at a society to be studied. In my investigation of lobstering as a modern industry, I focused on technical skills and issues concerning production and marketing. My particular interest in the management of common-property resources was sparked when I served as social anthropologist for the Fisheries Management Division of the National Marine Fisheries Service in 1974–75.

To gather material for this book I interviewed more than 190 fishermen along the central coast, many in their homes or on the docks. Many others took me and my research assistants out in their boats and put up with innumerable questions and the slowing of their fishing operations as we recorded data on the catches. Several deserve my special thanks: Woodbury Post and Eugene Witham of Owls Head; Burt Witham of Tenants Harbor; Doug Anderson of Port Clyde; Phil Davis of Pleasant Point; Maynard Winchenback of Friendship; Teddy Palino and Ken Prior of Bremen; Edgar Drisko, Norman Davis, Fred Boyington, Kendall Fossett, and Bryan Sawyer of New Harbor; Jimmy Bracket, George Cushing, Russ Nesbit, Brian McClain, and Dan Chaney of Pemaquid Harbor; Rusty Court of Monhegan and Boothbay; Charlie Begin of Boothbay; and Bob Green of Orrs Island. They are among the best fishermen in the state, and to almost every project I have undertaken they have contributed reams of information, much of it over the roar of a heavy diesel engine at sea.

Two of my former students made special contributions. Mary Ann Bates, when she was an undergraduate, provided a great deal of information and insight into the kinship system and the "local sociology." She has since moved from informant to professional and is enrolled in the doctoral program in anthropology at the University of Massachusetts. The second is Tim Staples, who has gone lobstering since childhood, has served as manager of the Swans Island Fisherman's Cooperative, and is currently a lobster buyer for a large wholesale firm in Portland. Tim gave special insights into the marketing system and cooperatives.

I am also indebted to biologists Jim Thomas (now retired), of the Maine Department of Marine Resources, and Tom Morrissey of the National Marine Fisheries Service.

I owe special thanks to Jayne Lello and Dr. John Bort, who were my research associates from 1977 through 1978. University of Maine faculty members Jim Wilson, Ralph Townsend, and Bob Bayer, who have also studied various aspects of the lobster and lobster industry, have provided insights, ideas, and criticism over the years. Toby Lazarowitz and I wrote two unpublished papers on kinship. Many of our ideas appear in chapter 2. Cathy Brann prepared the three line drawings and Steve Bicknell drew the maps and printed the photographs. Several people made extensive comments on the final draft of this book: Rod Forsgren and Ted Holmes, who are on the faculty of the University of Maine and who have been professionally connected with the lobster industry; Elizabeth Shaw, a peerless editor; anthropologist Courtland Smith; and historian Nathan Lippert. Charles Backus and Jeff Grathwohl of the University Press of New England did a good deal to turn my manuscript into a book. Finally, I offer my most sincere thanks to my wife, Dr. Ann Acheson, a fellow anthropologist, who proofread and commented on several drafts of this book.

Orono, Maine   J.M.A.
November 1987

The Lobster Gangs
of Maine

Introduction

High risk and uncertainty, in all parts of the world, are the everyday lot of the fisherman. The sea is a dangerous and alien environment, one in which man is poorly equipped to survive. Zones of marine life typically contain very large numbers of species that require different and highly specific fishing techniques. Even when those techniques are effectively applied, the abundance of a particular species can fluctuate wildly in ways that both fishermen and biologists find difficult to predict. On shore, there also seems to be as little logic or consistency in market prices, which means that a good catch does not always equal a good day's income.

This book focuses on what happens at sea and in the harbor communities of one very interesting segment of the fishing industry—Maine lobstering. While fishermen cannot control the sea, the wind, or the concentration of fish, they are able to reduce some of the uncertainty of the business of fishing through a variety of networks, community institutions, and individual strategies. Survival in the Maine lobster-fishing industry depends on ties with fellow lobstermen, the ability to negotiate with lobster dealers, and the sharing of certain skills.

Given the stereotype of the Maine lobster fisherman, this emphasis on social obligations and networks may seem out of place. In

American folklore, the Maine lobster fisherman often appears as the last of the rugged individualists. He is his own boss and his own man, willing to defend his independence with violence if necessary. His daily activities are dictated by weather and the turn of the seasons rather than by the office clock, governmental bureaucracy, or society's expectations. Fishermen tend to present themselves to tourists as men who earn their living from a relentless and icy sea with nothing but their skill, courage, and tenacity. If sophisticated urbanites chuckle at the rustics on the Maine docks, they do so with a tinge of envy, for the lobster fishermen embodies many of our most cherished virtues. He is, along with the farmer and rancher, the quintessential American.

There is some truth in these stereotypes. The lobster fisherman does own his own firm and usually is able to set his own schedule. A man who cannot operate a boat and handle his fishing gear alone at sea does not last long in the business. Yet on the whole, such stereotypes are misleading. They obscure the fact that the lobster fisherman is caught up in a thick and complex web of social relationships. Survival in the industry depends as much on the ability to manipulate social relationships as on technical skills.

In recent years, some social anthropologists have turned their attention to the topic of work and the social organization of industry. It has become apparent that each industry has a set of traditions, rules of behavior and myths about itself. Those of the lobster fishery of central Maine are perhaps more colorful than most. In this book I seek to describe the subculture and social organization of lobster fishermen and the way this organization is adapted to the social and physical environment.

Maine lobster fishermen live in long-established communities, interact with other people from "town," and are concerned primarily with events in their own community. These communities are inextricably tied to the state, the region, and the nation. They share an enormous number of social and cultural traits with other fishing communities in the United States and throughout the world. But the relevant social unit for most fishermen is not the fishing industry as a whole; it is the men fishing for the same species with the same gear in the same area. They share skills and a common knowledge of the means to exploit and market a certain product. When lobstermen meet, conversation inevitably revolves around such specific topics. Members of these lobster-fishing communities interact a great deal, both in person and on the radio. Although they are direct competitors, lobstermen are the most useful people in one another's lives. Indeed, they often stress the differences in behavior and attitudes among men fishing for other species. Typically, they view the men in their own fishery as harder working and more virtuous than those who catch other types of fish for a living.

In many other fisheries throughout the world, fishermen exploiting the same species in the same area exchange valuable information and serve as yardsticks of success for one another. Courtland Smith (personal communication 1977) states that the Oregon fishermen who seek the same species are a "community"; Fredrik Barth (1966) notes such units, which he calls "clusters," among Norwegian fishermen. For Maine lobstermen, I use the term "harbor gang" to refer to such clusters because these social units are composed of the lobster fishermen from the same harbor. Clusters in each type of fishery have certain unique features.[1] The most distinctive feature of lobstering clusters or harbor gangs is that they claim and defend fishing areas. Territoriality does not exist in any other Maine fishery.

The men in each gang are involved in an elaborate dancelike interaction in which cooperation must be balanced with competition, secrecy with openness, and sharing with self-interest. Smith (personal communication 1987) has pointed out that "the social obligations and networks of lobstermen manage a complex set of variables."

Although women hold 9 percent of the lobstering licenses (Martin and Lipfert 1985: 118), only a handful fish on their own on a full-time basis. More serve as helpers (sternmen) for their husbands and fathers. Many appear to hold licenses as insurance against the day when entry into the industry may be limited by law and licenses become rare and expensive. People on the Maine coast talk about "lobstermen" and "fishermen," and I will follow local convention. However, the future may well see the word "lobsterman" become an inaccurate anachronism as the number of women in the industry increases, which it almost certainly will. Currently women are far from inactive. Many keep the books and handle dozens of other business matters while their husbands are at sea.

The Lobster Industry

Lobsters have been part of the New England diet since early colonial times. The English settlers who came to the Popham colony off the mouth of Kennebec River in 1607 reported that they gaffed fifty lobsters for food within an hour. Captain John Smith of Virginia, who visited Monhegan and midcoast Maine in the early 1600s, enthusiastically described the plenitude of lobsters that could be taken in any bay. The lobsters were said to be of enormous size, some measuring up to five feet long. Lobsters were available in abundance in the markets of colonial New York and Boston. A big lobster could be bought for a "penny half-penny" in Boston in the 1740s.

Real commercial exploitation of the lobster, however, did not begin until much later. Unlike most other kinds of fish, lobsters must be shipped alive. Uncooked, dead lobsters develop toxins that will sicken and possibly kill anyone who eats them. As a result, the lobster industry in its present form did not begin until the development of the lobster smack—a sailing vessel with seawater tanks in its hold, which made it possible to ship lobsters to East Coast markets inexpensively. The first smacks were developed in Long Island Sound in the late 1700s, and smackmen gradually moved up the coast. They began operating in southern Maine in the early 1820s and became common along the central coast in the 1840s (Martin and Lipfert 1985: 13).

The industry was given a further boost by the development of lobster canning in Gloucester. One factory at Harpswell, owned by the Underwood Corporation, was canning lobsters by 1844. By the 1880s, five firms owned dozens of canning plants on the Maine coast, packing clams, corn, fish, and shellfish. In 1880, twenty-three of these plants packed lobster (Goode 1887b: 695, 687).

During these decades, lobster fishing was a part-time, seasonal activity, done in the spring and the fall by men and boys whose primary occupations were farming or other forms of fishing. No fishing was done in winter, when storms threatened the small boats, or in the middle of the summer, when lobsters were shedding and thought to be unfit for consumption. Lobsters were easy to catch. A part-time fisherman could get between one thousand and two thousand lobsters a month. At two or three cents each, they were quickly converted into a respectable sum of money for the times. It is little wonder that lobstering spread rapidly along the coast, and that by the 1860s, every Maine harbor seems to have had its fleet.

The lobster industry has experienced marked ups and downs. Cape Cod supplied all of the lobster for the East Coast urban market in the early nineteenth century, but by 1812 that fishery showed signs of decline and was almost nonexistent by the 1880s (Ackerman 1941: 43). Supplies of lobsters were so low in the 1840s that buyers and smackmen turned to Maine. By the 1880s, the Maine lobster catch was also down, and the size of lobsters had declined considerably. Industry buyers then went to Nova Scotia and other areas. By 1900 there were more than seven hundred canneries in the maritime provinces of Canada.

The cause of this precipitous decline was the rapacity of the canners, who preferred big lobsters when they could get them but would take anything in a pinch. By 1880, the Maine canneries were canning small "snappers"—many of them half-pound lobsters—which probably damaged the breeding stock. (The smallest legal lobster today weighs over a pound.)

The response to the imminent destruction of the lobstering industry was regulation. In 1872, Maine enacted a law prohibiting the taking of females bearing eggs. Two years later, it became illegal to take lobsters under 10.5 inches overall, and even more drastic, the fishery was closed between August 1 and October 15. The closed season, in combination with the minimum-length law and declining productivity of the canneries, made canning lobsters far less profitable than it had been. Lobster canning had ceased in Maine by 1895.

In the past century, the lobster catch has proven remarkably steady. The maximum annual catch during the last decades of the nineteenth century was 25 million pounds in 1898. Since World War II, catches of lobsters have ranged from 15.9 million pounds in 1948 to 22.8 million pounds in 1965 (Townsend and Briggs 1982: Table A-11). A notable dip was recorded in the Depression, however. The catch was only 5 million pounds. It is not clear what caused this dip. Some people report that there was a good deal of overexploitation by fishermen desperate to make a living, but low prices also played a role. Prices fell to three cents per pound in the middle of the Depression, which made the occupation very unprofitable. In all probability, there were fewer lobsters to catch in this period, and even fewer surviving lobstermen to catch them.

In the late 1980s, the lobster stock appears to be stable, but fishermen are increasingly caught in a price squeeze. The number of fishermen, along with the number of traps, has increased; the same number of lobsters are being shared by more fishermen. Moreover, the prices fishermen receive for their catches have not kept pace with the costs of fuel, boats, and bait. The future may see fewer than the 2,200 full-time lobstermen now fishing.[2]

There is one bright light on the horizon. Fishermen and the Maine Lobstermen's Association have become serious about promulgating measures that might maintain the breeding stock and enable the lobster fishery to continue as a productive industry. Chapter 7 is concerned with strategies and adaptations toward this end.

CHAPTER I

Cycles

The Weather

Throughout the year, daily weather conditions in Maine are highly variable. Typically, a few good days with bright blue skies are followed by days of overcast or precipitation. Occasionally, a high or low weather system gets stalled over the state, bringing the same kind of weather for a week or two, but such situations are rare. Most of the year the adage holds: "If you don't like the weather, wait a day."

Midsummer weather is considered ideal. The days are warm—temperatures are usually in the seventies—and the nights, thanks to the waters of the Gulf of Maine (which never go over fifty-seven degrees), are always cool. The thermometer rarely reaches ninety degrees, and it is not uncommon for temperatures to drop into the low fifties or high forties. As a result, Maine has long been a refuge from summer heat for millions of city dwellers from southern New England and the Middle Atlantic states. Since the years following the Civil War, dozens of wealthy families have maintained summer estates in places such as Boothbay Harbor, Camden, and Bar Harbor.

Early in the summer, a fog bank seems to hover over the Gulf of Maine. When the wind comes from the south or the east, the fog

moves shoreward, engulfing the tips of the peninsulas and sometimes penetrating a few miles inland. On days when it is "thick a
fog," one often can see only a few feet ahead. Driving is hazardous,
and seamen navigate their boats primarily with instruments. When
the wind blows from the north or west, the fog bank retreats further
out to sea, but it is always out there if one goes far enough.

August and September bring the best sailing weather of the year.
The wind typically comes from the north and west, bringing crisp,
clear, windy days. Local people a generation ago called them "State
of Maine days."

As summer turns to fall, the days and nights turn cooler. The
leaves begin to turn colors in late September and the height of the
"foliage" season is usually about October 15 to 20 on the coast. By
November all of the leaves have fallen, and stormy and windy days
become more common. Along the coast snow can be expected from
December until late March. Winter storms sometimes bring the
powdered snow so valued by skiers on inland mountains, but all too
often they bring heavy, damp snow, freezing rain, or hail. January or
February may see such heavy rain that all the snow is washed away,
leaving bare ground until the next snowstorm. Midwinter storms
can last for days. Sometimes, the wind blows for a week at a time,
making fishing very difficult.

In my opinion, the worst time in coastal Maine is mid March
through the first week of April. This part of the year really is not
winter; it certainly is not spring either. It is mud season. The frost
coming out of the ground renders all driveways and unpaved roads a
soupy morass. Nothing has turned green yet, and what snow remains is dirty and grey. The melting snow leaves puddles everywhere and swells every river and stream in the region. Floods are not
uncommon.

The coastal weather finally turns nice about the last week of April
or the first week of May. Buds start to appear on the trees; a few early
flowers are in bloom; and the earth turns solid again. Nevertheless,
experienced gardeners do not plant before mid May, for frosts may
occur in the first two weeks of that month.

By the first of June, the weather is warm and everything is in full
bloom. The bitter cold of midwinter and the grey, dank weather of

early spring are memories. By the first week of June, the first tourists and young people are trying the waters of the ocean beaches, always an invigorating experience.

Throughout the year, the moderating influence of the Gulf of Maine makes the coastal weather cooler in the summer and warmer in the winter than inland weather. A motorist can notice some sharp differences within a few miles. In the winter, driving from Pemaquid Harbor to Damariscotta, a distance of twelve miles, an observer would see the thermometer drop as much as ten or fifteen degrees. Rain in Pemaquid is often snow in Damariscotta. In the summer, the coast is invariably cooler than a few miles inland.

The Gulf of Maine and Its Fisheries

The Gulf of Maine, one of the world's most prolific fishing grounds, is an almost completely enclosed body of water. Its landward boundary extends from the southernmost point of Nova Scotia northward along the Bay of Fundy and southwestward again along the coasts of New Brunswick, Maine, and Massachusetts to Cape Cod. Its seaward boundary is a long string of shallow banks and shoals. On the west, the gulf is bordered by Browns Bank; the southern border is Georges Bank and Nantucket Shoals. The only deep-water connection into the gulf is the Northeast Channel, which separates Browns Bank from Georges Bank. Georges Bank, a major fishing ground, is less than two hundred feet deep in most places and in spots is much shallower. (See map 1.)

The Gulf of Maine is punctuated by a complicated series of small shoals and deep basins. Although these intermediate sets of banks cannot compete with the productivity of Georges Bank, together they produce many millions of pounds of fish each year. Moreover, these inshore and intermediary banks are the prime fishing grounds for small vessels operating from the ports of midcoastal Maine. Vessels from this region regularly fish on the Cashes Ledge and Jeffrey's Ledge. Only the largest vessels ever visit Georges Banks, which is well over a hundred miles from the midcoast harbors.

The high productivity of these fisheries results from a combina-

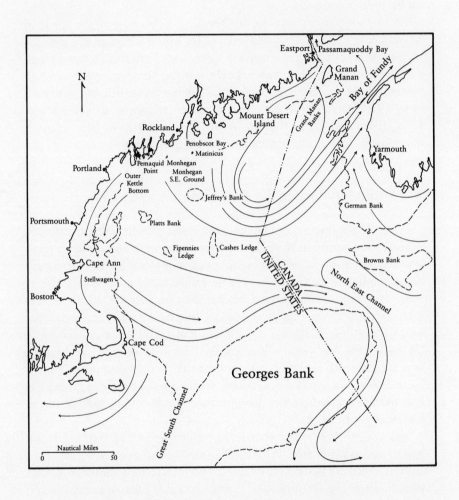

Map 1. Major fishing grounds and currents of the Gulf of Maine

tion of factors, including temperature, depth, bottom material, currents, and food supply. Ultimately, the size of fish stocks depends on the production of microorganisms, particularly photoplankton, which form the bottom of the food chain and live within a few feet of the surface because they require light. They also require nutrients in the form of dissolved carbon and minerals, which are most abundant on the coastal ocean bottom. Consequently, the most productive fisheries in the world are found in the shallow, coastal waters where upwelling currents bring nutrient-rich waters to the surface, providing food for the myriads of plankton.

Conditions in the Gulf of Maine are almost ideal for the production of fish. Several large rivers flow into the gulf: the Kennebec, the Penobscot, and the Saint John. Large amounts of fresh and salt water mix in the estuarine areas of these rivers, creating a concentration of nutrients that support a large population of larvae and small fish. In addition, the waters of the gulf not only flow horizontally but mix vertically as well. The surface waters flow counterclockwise in an elliptical pattern. Close to shore, currents flow southwest along the Maine and New Hampshire coast and then flow northeastward from Cape Cod to Nova Scotia and the Bay of Fundy. In several places, extensive vertical mixing is produced by the inshore movement of heavy, salty water and the countervailing movement of surface water (Apollonio 1979: 33). One such area of "upwelling" is off the southeastern coast of Nova Scotia; another occurs along the Maine coast between Grand Manan and Matinicus Island. These currents have important effects on the distribution of eggs, larvae, juvenile fish, and plankton.

In the 1980s the most important fisheries in Maine were lobster, groundfish, herring, scallops, and soft-shell clams. By any economic measure, lobster was the most important. In 1981, the latest year for which published records exist, Maine fishermen landed 22.6 million pounds of lobster, accounting for 43.7 percent of the value of all species landed. In 1980, 2,246 men identified their major fishery as lobster, and more than nine thousand lobster licenses were issued (Acheson et al. 1980: 256).

Either groundfish or the herring fishery ranks second in importance depending on the criteria being used. In 1981, 206 million pounds of groundfish were caught. The most valuable species are haddock, cod, pollock, and flounder, which accounted for 19.6 percent of the value of all fish caught in Maine during that year. Only 579 fishermen identified groundfish as their major fishery. The landed value of the herring catch, by way of contrast, was only $6.4 million, slightly less than 6 percent of the value of all species landed. The total value, however, of the canned and processed herring from the seventeen canning plants was $44 million in 1982 (Townsend and Briggs 1982: 176). Of still less importance are scallops and clams, although the revenues generated by these two fisheries remain significant.

Virtually every harbor on the Maine coast has at least a dozen boats fishing for lobsters most of the year. Lobstering is particularly important in small harbors along the central coast; vessels devoted to groundfish and herring are concentrated in the larger harbors and ports. In Maine, lobstering is a day fishery, carried on close to shore by men working alone or in pairs, in boats between thirty and forty feet long and within ten miles of shore. The few lobstermen who fish the offshore banks of the gulf use larger boats and devote full-time to this endeavor.

Lobster Biology

The American lobster (*Homarus americanus*) is a hard-shelled crustacean that lives on the ocean bottom in the waters off the Atlantic coast between Newfoundland and the Carolinas. (See figure 1.) Adult lobsters can be found in depths from 6 to 1,200 feet. The concentrations of lobsters are greatest, however, in depths less than 180 feet, either along the shores or in shoal areas. Lobsters tend to inhabit rocky bottom, especially where there is a great deal of kelp, possibly because of the camouflage it provides.

Lobsters eat a wide variety of foods, including living and dead organisms. The preferred foods are apparently fish, mollusks, and small crustaceans. They can also filter plankton and small organisms from the water and thus live in untended traps for considerable periods. Lobsters are cannibalistic and will attack smaller lobsters and soft-shelled ones of any size. Because cannibalism is particularly

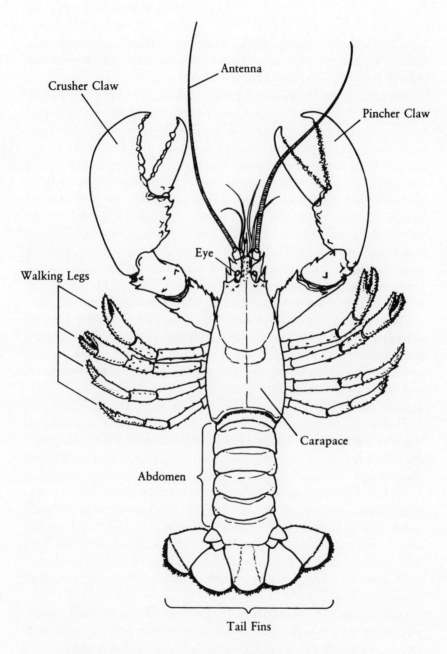

Figure 1. The American lobster (*Homarus americanus*)

common when the creatures are crowded together in captivity, fishermen, dealers, and pound operators must separate soft-shelled and
injured lobsters from the others.

When the lobster's body has grown beyond the limits of its shell,
molting, or "shedding," occurs. During shedding, the lobster shell
splits along the bottom of the carapace, and the lobster wiggles out
of its shell, which remains intact. During the next few days, the entire lobster is very soft and weak. Touching one at this stage is rather
like touching gelatin covered with a paper-thin shell. This shell begins to harden within a few days. While the shell is soft, the lobster's
only defense is to hide among the rocks. Most lobsters molt between
June and August, although molting can occur in any month. The period from mid June to mid July is very poor for lobstering, because
large numbers of lobsters are in hiding. Very small lobsters apparently molt several times annually, but the commercial-size lobsters,
which are at least seven years old, ordinarily molt only once a year.

Mating can occur only after molting, when the female is soft and
defenseless. The male lobster deposits sperm in the female's seminal
receptacle, where it remains until the eggs are mature, which may
not be for a year. As many as fifty thousand ripe eggs are extruded
and glued to the female's abdominal appendages until they hatch,
usually the following summer. Some female lobsters become sexually mature when they reach between 3.1 and 3.5 inches (80 and 90
mm) on the carapace, but in Maine, 50 percent do not mature until
they are 3.5 to 3.7 inches (90 to 95 mm). Males are mature at a much
smaller size (1.8 to 2.8 inches [45 to 70 mm]) (Krouse 1972, 1973).

Because lobsters require highly saline water, they are not found in
numbers up rivers or in estuarine areas with large influxes of fresh
water. Water temperature affects migration, growth, survival, and
catches. Research suggests that the production of marketable lobster
(recruitment) will be largest when mean annual sea temperatures
are between 48 and 52 degrees Fahrenheit (9 and 11 degrees centi-
grade) (Dow 1969: 1062–63).

Older tagging studies indicate that lobsters do not migrate seasonally; later work suggests that relatively localized migratory movements are common in the central coast area. Some lobsters do
migrate longer distances. They generally travel in a southwesterly
direction, apparently because of the counterclockwise coastal cur-

rents. Whatever the mechanisms, lobsters are caught in different locations in different seasons. In winter, when onshore waters are very
cold, the animals are best trapped in warmer water over 30 fathoms
(180 feet). In late spring and early summer, as the waters warm near
shore, lobsters can best be caught closer in, often within feet of
breaking surf. During the summer molting season, when lobsters
stay among the rocks for protection, they are difficult to catch at all.

The Annual Round

The annual round of full-time lobster fishermen is influenced by
the biology of the lobster, the weather, involvement in other fisheries, and markets. Although every lobster fishing operation has its
unique features, the four seasons bring very different patterns of activity for most fishermen.

During the early summer, when large numbers of lobsters are
shedding their shells and hiding in the rocks, fishing is very poor and
catches fall dramatically. At this time, many lobstermen take their
traps out of the water and use the time to maintain their equipment
and paint their boats.

The late summer is a period of high fishing activity. The weather
is good, and lobsters are more available, since a new age class has
molted into legal size. Lobsters are very active in the warm summer
water and are thus easier to catch. As almost all the traps are placed
in the narrow strip of water close to shore or near shoals, traps are
crowded together. Congestion is further increased by skiff fishermen
and part-timers who normally operate only at this time of year.

During July and August the price of lobster is relatively high, because of the influx of hundreds of thousands of tourists into the
coastal regions.

Immediately after Labor Day, when there is little demand from
local restaurants and catches are large, prices typically drop to their
annual lows. At this time of year, many lobsters are not sold immediately but are stored in pounds to be sold during the winter when
the price is higher. Most pounds are formed by closing off a bay or
inlet and building a dam to allow circulation of seawater.

Fall and early winter are the most productive times of year for lobster fishermen. Catches are very good, and prices begin to climb during October and November. Lobsters begin to move into deeper water further offshore so that men are fishing in fifteen- to thirty-fathom water. Traps are less crowded because a larger area is exploited during this time of year. At this time, fishermen put in the water as many traps as possible and pull them every chance they get. Many men who normally fish alone hire sternmen between late August and Thanksgiving.

As the fall progresses, the increasing incidence of storms often prevents fishermen from tending their traps and can result in a large number of trap losses. After October no outboard-powered boats are used for fishing and small inboard-powered boats are not used after November.

Late winter and early spring are a period of marked inactivity. The weather is often so bad that fishermen cannot pull their traps for days on end. Lobsters are also rather inactive during this cold season and thus far less likely to be caught. The best fishing is in deep water three to ten miles from shore where inversion layers keep the water relatively warm. Fishermen must spend a lot of time getting to and from fishing grounds and must pull traps in waters exposed to the full force of the wind. The only attractions of winter fishing are higher prices paid for lobsters at this time of year. Despite the price, many men fish only a few days a month when the weather permits, devoting most of their time to building traps for the next season. Other fishermen cease fishing entirely and spend all their time maintaining equipment.

From the middle of April, as the water temperature warms, lobsters become more active and begin to migrate toward shore. Fishermen begin to pull their traps more often as the weather improves, and the number of lobsters caught increases. The end of April and first part of May usually see a rapid increase in both number of days fished and catches. During May, prices usually fall dramatically. Demand for lobsters is relatively weak, since there are few tourists, and the increase in catches tends to cause a short-term glut on the market. In previous years, men who went spring lobstering did well and could expect good catches for a few weeks in late April to the first week of June. Since the mid 1970s, spring lobstering has been very poor, apparently because most of the legal-size lobsters have been caught during the previous fall.

Increasingly, fishermen have been turning to other fisheries during the winter and spring. When shrimp are abundant, many lobstermen go shrimping from December to March. Others go scalloping or groundfishing during these months, depending on the price and availability of species. In the mid-1980s, it was not at all uncommon for fishermen to go lobstering in the prime months from August to December and to devote most of their time in winter, spring, and early summer to scalloping or shrimping. These cyclical changes can be seen in figure 2, which records the catches of one fisherman and the prices he received in 1968.

Two aspects of this seasonal cycle in catch and prices deserve emphasis. First, and most obvious, catch and price are inversely related. The price comes to its annual peak during February and March, when catches are at their annual low. Late summer and fall see the lowest prices of the year. Not only are lobsters plentiful, but, with the exodus of tourists, demand is relatively weak.

Second, fishermen are responding more to availability of lobsters than to price; that is, they maximize their effort in the late summer and fall, when lobsters are plentiful, and reduce it in the winter, even though lobster prices are at their annual high then. This strategy is perfectly rational from the fisherman's viewpoint. He makes far more money when lobsters are plentiful, even though the price is low, than he does in midwinter, when, despite high prices, a whole day's fishing might net only a few dozen lobsters.

The Daily Round

A lobsterman's day actually begins the previous night, when he decides whether the weather will allow fishing the next day. Fishermen are acute observers of the weather. Their own predictions are supplemented by radio and television reports. If a storm threatens, he may devote the day to doing tasks ashore, or running errands in one of the nearby cities. If the weather promises to be good, or is only mildly threatening, he may rise in the early hours of the morn-

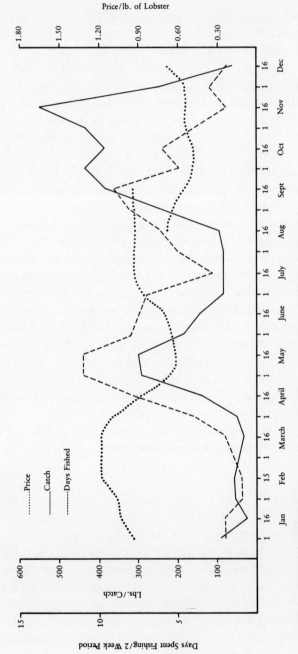

Figure 2. One Fisherman's average catch, prices received, and days fished, 1968. In late summer, dealers offer different prices for hard-shell and soft-shell lobsters. The hard-shell lobsters, which have not yet shed, bring a higher price, since they are packed with meat. As summer turns to fall, and most lobsters have shed, only one price is offered. This single price structure is maintained throughout the rest of the year.

ing, usually while it is still dark, to have breakfast and make a lunch. Some wives make a point of getting up to see their husbands off, but many sleep through their husbands' departures. The men go directly to the docks where their boats are moored. A few fishermen own their docks, but most use the docks of the dealer or cooperative where they sell their catch. If the weather is fair, they may leave the harbor with little delay. At other times, they may hang around the dock talking, drinking coffee, and joking. If it is very foggy or the wind is rising, men may stay on the docks for as long as two hours before deciding whether to go fishing or do something else for the day.

When they do go fishing, they row out to their boats, put on their boots, foul weather gear, and gloves, start the engine, and cast off. They may tie up to the dock for a few minutes to take on gas or bait, if they have not done so the night before.

They leave the harbor at high speed, motors roaring and wake churning out behind. In the warm months of the year, when traps are located near shore, fishermen may arrive in a few minutes at the first set of traps. In the winter months, when traps are generally in deep water, they may have to travel an hour or more to get to their strings. If the trip is a long one, the fisherman and his helper may drink a cup of coffee and carry on a shouted conversation over the roar of the engine.

When they arrive at the first trap, the engine is cut, and the buoy or toggle is pulled into the boat with a gaff. The warp, or rope, connecting the buoy and trap is then engaged in the wheel of the hydraulic trap hauler, which is started, pulling the trap rapidly to the surface. The spinning wheel of the hauler piles the warp in a mounting stack all over the working area of the cockpit, around and under the fisherman's feet, spewing seawater and slime about the cockpit. When the trap emerges from the water, the fisherman stops the hauler, pulls it into the boat, and puts it on the side or "rail." He quickly unties the small string that holds the door of the trap shut and removes the lobsters. Those clearly under the legal minimum are thrown overboard with little ado. The others are put in a bucket.

Next the fisherman cleans out any other animals that may have entered the trap, such as sea urchins and crabs, and rebaits the trap. If he is using fish frames (i.e., fish from which the fillets have been cut) as bait, he places them on the bait string using the baiting iron. If he is using bagged herring, alewives, or menhaden, he ties a filled bait bag inside the entryway of the trap and ties shut the trap door. Steering the boat to the site where he intends to place the trap, and taking into account the location of other traps with which he might become entangled, the depth, and other factors, the fisherman pushes the trap overboard. Speeding up the engine, he heads for the next trap, taking great care not to become entangled as the warp and buoy are flying out the stern of the vessel attached to the sinking trap. If the fisherman is fishing doubles or trawls, all of the traps attached to one warp line are cleaned out and rebaited, after which all the traps are put in the water at one time. When multiple traps are placed, the first one is tossed in the water, and the remaining traps are pulled off the rail after the moving boat. Where men are fishing doubles, the fisherman usually cleans and rebaits the first trap pulled, while the sternman does the second trap.

Between traps or strings, the fisherman measures the lobsters he believes are more than 3³⁄₁₆ inches on the carapace (eye socket to the back) using a brass gauge produced according to state legal requirements. The ones that prove to be too small are thrown over the rail. The fisherman must also discard all lobsters with eggs, or "notch-tailed" lobsters, which have had eggs in the past. The legal-size lobsters are placed in storage containers after their powerful crusher claws have been immobilized, either by "pegging" (pushing a spruce peg into the joint to prevent the lobster from opening his claw) or by placing a large elastic band around the claw. This procedure prevents cannibalism and protects anyone who must handle the lobsters. Fishermen store their catches on board in crates, bushel baskets, or barrels filled with running seawater.

The fisherman may pull between 150 and 500 traps in a day, going through the same procedure each time. There are few breaks in the day: the men may stop for coffee once or twice and take a few minutes in the late morning for lunch. Often, crews really do not stop working at all but drink a cup of coffee and eat a sandwich between strings of traps.

The daily routine rarely alters. A fisherman may move some traps, a procedure that needs to be done several times a year. The traps to be moved are pulled and stacked on the stern of the boat with the warps coiled and placed inside. They are either reset in different places or brought ashore to be dried and repaired.

In the warm months, plants and barnacles grow on the buoys and warp lines and must be removed periodically. Some men clean their buoys at sea by dunking them in a bucket filled with chlorine bleach or with water heated almost to the boiling point by the engine. Sea growth also dies when the traps are brought ashore and dried on the docks. Some men carry a few tools, nails, and wooden laths to make minor repairs on damaged traps. Fishermen usually have to stop several times a day to untangle traps. After a storm, when it is common for large numbers of traps to become entangled, straightening out gear can slow up work for several days.

To the casual observer, lobster fishing consists of nothing but the dull, uninterrupted routine of pulling the same traps day after day. To the fisherman, maneuvering the boat and pulling traps are simply mechanical tasks performed more or less automatically. Most of his attention is on the far more important job of deciding where to place traps to maximize catches and minimize losses and entanglements. His mind is on the sea bottom, considering the habits of the lobsters, as well as the weather and the strategies of other fishermen. He must also try to recall the locations of the hundreds of traps in dozens of strings spread over many miles of ocean. The only diversion on board is music. Many boats carry, in addition to citizen's band (CB) or very high frequency (VHF) radios, regular radios, which are tuned to country music stations.

After the last trap is pulled, the fisherman heads his boat for the harbor at high speed. While under way, the fisherman or his sternman begin cleaning up the boat, which is well begrimed with seaweed, slime, and an assortment of marine plants and animals. Most of the cleaning is done by scrubbing with a stiff brush and hosing off the dirt with seawater. Accumulated debris is shoveled over the side. The scrubbing and seawater, however, never completely remove the pungent smell of lobster bait that permeates the boat, the equipment, and the hands of fishermen.

At the harbor, the fisherman goes directly to the wharf of the dealer or cooperative to sell his catch. The lobsters are first weighed by the dock attendant or manager and packed in crates. Some dealers pay their fishermen in cash, but more often they issue a receipt and pay by check through the mail. While at the dock, the fisherman may also buy gas and bait. He then puts his boat on the mooring, rows to shore, and goes directly home. Ordinarily there is little tarrying on the dock after a long day of fishing.

During the height of the fishing season, many fishermen may work from dawn to dark, but at other times of the year they arrive home in the middle or late afternoon after only seven to nine hours on the water. Men strongly prefer to start work in the early morning, when the sea is usually calm, and end early, before the winds pick up and the seas become rougher. Rough weather increases the difficulty of finding and rebaiting traps. A fisherman with a nine-to-five schedule would find it far more difficult to pull as many traps as a man who starts before sunup. After arriving home, most fishermen do an errand or two connected with their fishing business. Following supper they might call friends to swap information on prices, catches, and the weather, and finally, before going to sleep, turn on the radio for news of wind and weather.

CHAPTER 2

Kinship and Community

Midcoastal Maine saw its economic heyday in the first half of the nineteenth century. Based on the thriving lumber, shipbuilding, and fishing industries, the populations of Bristol, Waldoboro, Friendship, and Saint George peaked between 1860 and 1880. After 1880, a long period of decline began. All the regions' basic industries faltered in the years following the Civil War. As other parts of the country became more attractive—with the opening of the West and the fluorescence of industry in the Middle Atlantic states—people began to leave midcoastal Maine. By the 1880s the region was well on its way to becoming what it is today—a quiet, rural place on the margins of the urban, industrialized parts of the East Coast. The population reached its lowest point in 1940 and has since been climbing slowly, because of the influx of retirees and tourists. Increasingly, the midcoast is becoming a retirement colony, and every town now has dozens—if not hundreds—of older people who live in winterized cottages and remodeled houses along the shore. Most of these people are from out of state. Men who are no longer part of the labor market often outnumber fishermen whose roots in the area often go back for generations. Aside from the Bath Iron Works, which has some six thousand employees, and the cement plant in Thomaston, tourism and fishing are now the largest industries in the small midcoastal towns.

Visitors to Maine coastal communities are quickly made to feel the difference between themselves and the long-term residents. Some visitors have commented that they felt more like aliens than guests of the aloof Mainers. People who have moved to these towns from outside come to realize that they will never be able to participate fully in the local way of life.

The divisions within these communities are complicated and cannot be understood until we know a good deal about the attitudes, values, and social organization of the long-term residents. It is important to note that "outsiders" include not only the casual tourists, but also the hundreds of summer people who reside in the cottages lining the shore, along with the "newcomers," virtually all retired folk and other latter-day arrivals who live in town throughout the year. In the summer months, these coastal regions are largely inhabited by people who are not "full" members of the community, if indeed they are members at all.

Outsiders can become full members of the community, but this is rare. More often, community members and outsiders live in different social worlds and ignore one another. Communication between them is minimal and superficial. "Cottage owners" rarely entertain members of the other groups, and only a few (somewhat scandalous) intermarriages have taken place. Summer families who have owned cottages for generations may really know only one or two "local people."

The people living on both sides of this divide view one another with a mixture of humor and hostility. Both outsiders and community members joke about their opposite numbers. "Visitors" tell jokes about Maine people akin to the Polish jokes of the Midwest or the "Newfie" jokes of Canada. The more extreme of these have as their staples bears, cold winters, isolation, and silent, hostile people who, it is suggested, are the products of rampant incest. On numerous occasions I have heard cottage owners and tourists describe Maine in the most uncomplimentary terms. Many felt, with some justification, that they had been lied to and cheated by local tradespeople and merchants. Maine people retaliate in kind: "I had an awful dream last night. I dreamed my own car had a Massachusetts license plate on it." At times the hostility between the two subcultures is palpable. One T-shirt slogan seen around the coast not long ago reads "I am not a tourist. I live here, and I don't answer any questions," a statement that clearly does not offer the hand of a friendship. More hostile Maine humor about visitors features ethnic, religious, and racial stereotypes worthy of the Ku Klux Klan.

Community members do not have a universally accepted name for themselves. They may speak of "local people" or "natives" but more often simply "us" or "we." Summer visitors have a variety of names for themselves: "tourists," "cottage owners," or "summer people," among others. The names that members of the two divisions call each other in private are less than complimentary. Local people speak of "summer complaints," "tourassts," "people from away," and "rusticators." Outsiders in turn refer to community members as "locals" or "natives," or if they choose to be nasty, as "townie trash" or "local scum."

In great part, the hostility between community members and outsiders has its roots in social class differences. Community members by and large come from a lower social stratum than do many of the outsiders. Cottage owners are often quite wealthy, coming from the upper or upper-middle class of urban areas. Many recent residents are retired from professions or business. Many community members feel, and with some reason, that the tourists are patronizing and condescending. The tourists often believe they are treated curtly and rudely. Infrequently, long-term friendships develop between community members and outsiders, but on the whole, Maine towns, especially in the summer, are not melting pots but plural societies, split down the middle by a complicated ethnic boundary.

Towns, Hamlets, and Associations

Practically all fishermen are full members of the community, and if we want to understand the world of the lobster fisherman, we must concentrate on the social and cultural aspects of the "inner" communities. Despite their many links with the outside world, the fishing towns of central Maine and their permanent residents are closely knit.[1] To many of the community members, the town is the most important social unit in their lives. Most of the important social contacts are within the towns, and the inhabitants' attention focuses inward on their home community to a large degree. There are very few institutions within the coastal towns, but those that do exist assume an importance difficult to overestimate in the lives of the permanent residents. For so-called natives, the most significant institutions are the residential units, local community, voluntary associations, and kinship.

Although town and hamlet are both important units to Maine coastal people, they serve different functions, dominating different spheres of activities. Towns are political units. According to state law, only the towns—not the hamlets—have a right to tax, organize school systems, elect public officials, hire police, and pass ordinances and enforce them. The towns are usually run by selectmen, who are elected for one- to three-year terms; a few of the larger towns have town managers. All major decisions, including appropriations, are made by majority vote at annual town meetings. Most of the tax money is spent on schools and roads. Few of the fishing towns have police departments, and most have only volunteer fire departments. Ordinarily, any attempts to expand governmental functions or bureaucracy beyond these elementary institutions are resoundingly defeated. The towns are able to practice minimal government because the state of Maine provides an enormous range of services. The township is the unit of identity in any activity relating to local political power or to town-financed institutions such as schools and the fire department. People belong to the town fire department, their children go to the town schools, and they blame the town selectmen for raising taxes and maintaining the roads poorly.

Townships are not physically distinct units, however, in the way that hamlets are. Each hamlet is a separate cluster of houses and buildings, clearly separated from other hamlets by fields and woods. There are sometimes miles of woods between hamlets in the same township. Almost everyone who lives in a particular hamlet knows everyone else, and most friendships arise within hamlets. Not all people in hamlets are friends by any means. In some cases people in the same hamlet have not been in certain houses for thirty years.

When asked by outsiders where they live or what their address is, few people respond with the name of the township. Rather, they name a particular hamlet—Round Pond, New Harbor, or Port Clyde, for example. Even the telephone directory reinforces this identification with hamlets, for names, telephone numbers, and mailing addresses are listed by hamlet. During my fieldwork, my family's mail came to the Pemaquid Harbor (hamlet) post office, and we were listed in the phone book under Pemaquid Harbor. Like good natives, we said we lived in "Pemaquid Harbor."

Social distance increases with distance from one's own hamlet. Within the hamlet, inhabitants feel perfectly at home. People in townships also feel an identity with those in their own town, even though they might not know everyone there intimately. People from different towns, however, feel a marked sense of distance mixed with a little hostility and even fear, which is expressed in unfortunate name calling and stereotypes.

Talking about the people in a neighboring town, one fisherman said: "They are just a little weird. They keep to themselves and have a lot of feuds over nothing. They are backward in a lot of ways." Another, speaking of a different town, said: "They are a bunch of outlaws. They have a couple of bars and it is like the Old West in there. Even the police are afraid to come into town. If they don't like what the first selectman does, they'll go punch him out." Such informants often back up their statements with specific though apocryphal stories. The implication is, of course, that these incidents always happen in neighboring towns—not their own.

Such negative feelings, it should be noted, appear to be directed at people from nearby townships. People from more distant towns rarely interact and hold only the vaguest ideas about one another. The geography of the region helps to promote these feelings of isolation. Towns on other peninsulas may be only five to fifteen miles away by boat but are often an hour or more by car.

Much of the social and cultural life of Maine coastal communities revolves around a plethora of voluntary organizations. Some have only five to ten members, while others may have a hundred or more on file. In the town of Bristol in 1980, there were five recreational clubs (e.g., the Fish and Game Club), five fraternal organizations (Masons, Odd Fellows, Red Men, Lions, Order of the Eastern Star), and five service and charitable organizations, including the volunteer fire department. The Veterans of Foreign Wars and the Daughters of the American Revolution had local chapters, and there was a local company of militia. Another six organizations were devoted to educational and cultural activities. There were also three Protestant churches and eight clubs associated with them: Bible-study groups, youth fellowships, a variety of men's and women's groups, and scout troops. There were also two fishermen's cooperatives, a chapter of the Grange, and a local business boosters' association.

All of these organizations drew most of their members from within the township itself; some of the smaller service or charitable organizations were composed of people from only one hamlet within the township. Only rarely did residents from other townships join these organizations.

In Bristol, as elsewhere in the region, voluntary associations provide an important social outlet. Moreover, a good deal of community service is performed by members of certain voluntary organizations, services that in larger cities and towns are provided by public agencies. Of particular importance in this regard are the volunteer fire department, the Friends of the Library, the associations supporting historic sites, and the business boosters.

The number, variety, and vitality of organizations in towns with such small permanent populations are amazing to new residents. The operation and activities of these organizations are buttressed by "local" political ideology, which strongly supports the ideal of volunteerism and local control.

In the 1970s, a local association was formed in one town to erect a building and to offer children recreational opportunities similar to those available in urban YMCAs. When the building was finished, the *Lincoln County News* quoted one of the association organizers as saying there had been "no federal funds, no state funds—just hard work and the community pulling toward one goal." This quotation captures local sentiment well.

Though local people and newcomers both have a high degree of participation in voluntary organizations, they are involved with different groups. Locals tend to be affiliated with fraternal, military, and church organizations; the newcomers are far more involved with cultural organizations and service clubs.

Fishermen, including those in the lobster fishery, are no exception to this pattern. In Bristol, of the seventy-nine people we interviewed, 56.9 percent were members of two to five different organizations.[2] The largest number belonged to the Veterans of Foreign War and the American Legion; church groups came next. Only one fisherman reported belonging to a cultural or educational club.

Fishermen and other local people often stressed during interviews that local clubs and associations were being taken over by outsiders and other newcomers who wanted to run the town and everything in it. Fishermen, one was led to believe, were being pushed out of local organizations. Such statements came across more as expressions of hostility toward newcomers than as statements of fact. Not only do fishermen and other local people have a relatively high rate of membership in associations, but they also dominate a large number of churches, fraternal organizations, military organizations, and the fire department. Fishermen are vociferous in commenting on any community activity affecting the waterfront, fishing, or ocean resources.

Kinship

Kin and the networks among them are the most important units in the lives of long-term residents. To a large extent, a person's feelings of worth, identity, and place in the social fabric are tied up with groups of local kin.

Kin groups are very large and involve a complicated set of ties. The density of kinship ties was illustrated when a long-term resident was asked to judge a grammar-school art contest. She accepted but said, "I probably should have disqualified myself since I am related to almost every child here." Two other women, also members of "old families," announced that they were equally related. None was exaggerating.

Kin meet on the job and visit back and forth constantly, often on a daily basis. Of course, in any given year, funerals, weddings, baptisms, and other rituals bring family members together. More important, kinship ties can be used to achieve access to a variety of valued goals.

In the study of kinship the objective genealogical facts are less significant than the interpretation and use of the kinship system by the people involved in it. After all, the facts about procreation are the same everywhere in the world. Any given person has two parents, four grandparents, eight great-grandparents, and so on. Theoretically, any person can trace genealogical ties, however distant, to any other person who has ever lived, yet no one does so, for obvious reasons. Forgetting kin is a practical necessity. Thus, in studying kinship, we need to ask: Which people are recalled as kin? What duties and obligations does an individual have in relation to people in various kinship statuses? Underlying these concerns is the realization that to a great extent we select our kin from a larger pool of potential relatives. We create our kinship past with certain contemporary aims in mind.

Kinship on the central coast of Maine is a variant on the bilateral kindred system found throughout the English-speaking world. Kindreds are essentially linked units of nuclear families.[3] Any individual has direct links to the family into which he or she was born, the spouse's family, and families that offspring might establish. Each of these different nuclear families has larger sets of linkages to other sets of families. In the United States as a whole, the recognition of nuclear family linkages tends to be narrow. In midcoastal Maine, it is far wider, with many individuals having an active knowledge of families linked through a common ancestor three or four generations in the past.

Who are the people likely to be defined as kin in Maine coastal towns?[4] In general they are the same people in the same categories selected as kin anywhere in the English-speaking world. There are some unusual twists and emphases, however.

Virtually all of the informants exhibited two forms of kinship memory. The first was a thin thread of kinship links into the distant past. The second was a bilateral network of contemporary kin, which extended five generations at most. This has been referred to as "the Christmas tree effect" by one famous student of American kinship

(Schneider 1968: 67–68). That is, the current kin recalled in detail are like the base of the tree. They stem from an ancestor alone at the top of the pyramid, like the star on the Christmas tree.

Our informants could not recall anyone farther back than their great-grandparents. However, most placed great emphasis on relating to some mythical ancestor who lived in the area or at least somewhere in the American colonies—not in England or any other European country. People who came over on the *Mayflower*, revolutionary generals, famous politicians, or the first settlers in the town were most often selected as the "famous ancestor." Most informants could not trace the exact set of linkages between themselves and this forebear, but the exact family history was unimportant. Merely knowing that they had that kind of connection to the past was what counted. In many cases, even though people could not recall the names of distant relatives, they were positive that the relatives had been born in the town and had resided there. In all cases, the emphasis was on locality, not lineality. In recounting relatives, there was some bias toward selecting kin in the male line because of a common surname, but people did not hesitate to trace ancestry through a female line if this procedure would link them to a famous ancestor, avoid linkages to a family or relative of "no account," or make some other point.

At the start of these thin threads into the past were elaborate units of more contemporary kin. People recalled their own sibling groups (brothers, sisters, their spouses, their children), as well as the sibling groups of spouses and parents. They recalled, on the whole, most of the people in their grandparents' generation. They often could not recall linkages such as third cousins, which would mean recalling their great-grandparents' generation in detail. In some cases, they never knew the names of these kin; in other cases they knew who they were but forgot to include them. People who had the same last name but were beyond the second-cousin range were identified as relatives, although informants could not specify what the link was and did not care.

Proximity played a big role in the kinship memory. Informants commonly recalled every single relative, including children, who lived in the same town or adjacent towns within a half-hour ride, and they knew a tremendous amount about these people. In no instance did informants fail to name a relative within the second-cousin range who lived in the same town or within ten miles. When kin moved away, however, they were quickly forgotten by many of their relatives. One college-educated informant could name neither the fiancée of her brother in New Jersey nor her first cousin's husband, even though the family lived in Bangor, about an hour and a half away. We saw this pattern repeatedly. Members of nuclear families were not forgotten by other members regardless of how far away they might move. People maintained ties with sons and daughters in Alaska and California. However, these migrants would quickly cease to be important to their first cousins and might not be recalled as "relatives" within the space of a few years.[5]

A woman is clearly a member of the family in which she was born until she marries. However, at marriage the kinship status of women becomes vague. While maintaining contact with consanguineal kin and taking a good deal of responsibility for aged parents and other close kin, a woman tends to identify and be identified with the family of her husband as time goes on. Thus older married women tend to be cut out of critical decisions and inheritance in their birth families. They are thought to have someone to "take care" of them, and they may even have left the area.

To a large extent, the reputation of any individual in the community is determined by the extended family from which he or she comes. Sometimes people talk about "good families" and "bad families," but usually the stereotypes about a family are far more specific and are phrased in terms of "blood" or inherited traits, which are thought to characterize whole family lines, a common idea in the English-speaking world (Strathern 1981: 162–41). In the fishing towns, family stereotypes usually emerge as a means of explaining the behavior of an individual. One family of good fishermen, for example, is known to "have a nose for fish"; another family is described as a bunch of "badlanders," meaning that everyone from the great-grandfather to his great-grandsons has had trouble with the law and has a reputation for heavy drinking.

Such characterization is a way of locking people into the past and explaining their present situation. The idiom of "blood" is often used in explaining success and failure. When an individual from an "unsuccessful" kin grouping obviously succeeds, the family stereotype rarely changes. That individual is seen as merely an exception to the rule. Sets of kin can, however, rise or fall in the esteem of their fellow townspeople, but such change takes time, and no single act of an individual will alter the total family reputation.

The reputation of a family—whether good or bad—is measured against a yardstick accepted by everyone in the community. Behind this yardstick is a whole value system and subculture. Although the characteristics of this system will be familiar to those acquainted with rural North America (Bennett 1969: 20ff.), a few local features might be emphasized. With a few variations, the value system is shared by both men and women.

In this highly utilitarian culture, reward is expected for honest effort. People who accept welfare or earn a living by manipulating others ("a slick talker") are scorned. Those who can solve practical problems are admired. Formal education for its own sake is not greatly valued, though education is more than acceptable if it helps a person to earn more money. Educated people who flaunt their education to demonstrate their superiority and who cannot cope with the practical problems of life are "educated fools." Independence and the ability to control one's own time are highly valued. The male's ideal is to own his own business. Conversely, men feel ashamed to take orders from someone else. For this reason, in Maine a man is never hired; he is merely "helping out." While a person is supposed to be independent, he or she is also expected to be helpful and cooperative in time of need. Though people should strive to succeed and to "better" themselves, a process defined almost totally in economic and political terms, overriding many of these values is an emphasis on equality and fair play. People are expected to be oriented toward their families and "do as well as possible for their children." Divorce, bearing children out of wedlock, providing inadequate support or care for children, all are disapproved of strongly, although in Maine, as in the rest of the United States, such behavior is not as strongly condemned as it has been in the past.

These values define "proper" behavior. Proper behavior, in combination with economic and political success, determines the family's prestige in the hierarchy. Only two to four families inhabit the pinnacle of the hierarchy. While there is no agreed-upon term for these families, every schoolchild knows who they are. Sometimes they are called the "look-up-to families." With the exception of a few professionals (lawyers, teachers), most of the prominent members of these kin units are owners of independent businesses. They usually own nice homes and good automobiles, duly noted in the town, although they do not live opulently by any means. On the bottom of the hierarchy are a few so-called poor families, living in low-quality housing; they may have no steady source of income and may even be on welfare. More important, members of these families may have criminal records, be involved in well-advertised drinking bouts, have children out of wedlock, and the like. In large measure, the earmarks of "successful" families are material goods; failure, however is defined primarily in terms of immoral behavior. Most family groupings lie somewhere in between. Of course, summer people and newcomers are not so measured, since they scarcely exist in the social universe.

While community members generally agree about the relative position of most families in the hierarchy, individuals may disagree about the position of a specific family. Several factors play a role in producing this differential perception. First, different informants have different knowledge. Relative newcomers in town tended to place one family very high on the status scale on the assumption that it was a "very old family." Another informant, who knew the family history in detail, placed it much lower, pointing out that it was relatively new to the township. Second, cultural variables by which behavior and worth are judged are inconsistent. The idea of equality and fair play can easily conflict with "success." Independence can conflict with the expectation of being cooperative. The education that leads to self-betterment can also lead to charges of snobbery. Finally, the actions of one family member must be weighed against the actions of other family members, past and present, in calculating the position of a family. One very hard working, friendly, and thoroughly decent man will never rise high in the estimation of his fellow townspeople: he works for someone else; two of his daughters were pregnant before marriage; and his brother is a convicted thief.

Membership in an established family gives a person a special niche in the social universe. Coming from a family that was first on the land gives a sense of belonging that can never be taken away. A person may live on a homestead owned by the family since the early 1800s. The names of family members may be recorded on monuments in the town square, and the offices they have held may be duly recorded in the annals of the township. These kinship units are not, however, simply cocoons that buffer the individual psychologically against the vagaries of fate; they also convey more tangible assets. Through the use of kinship ties, individuals can gain access to resources ranging from real estate and jobs to political support.[6] The nuclear family, kindred, and even ancestors long dead all have their uses and can be recalled at the appropriate moment.

The utility of kinship rests in large measure on the local ideology: "resources"—including jobs, land, and ocean access—should be reserved for local people. Since kinship and community are so closely linked, access to these resources is reserved for people from certain families. Outsiders who attempt to gain access are often ostracized. Community members, however, have a difficult time explaining why they should have preferential access. The notion of usufructuary rights is strong, as is the notion that resources should go to those who need them. People believe that those who control such assets should not give them to outsiders because of an obligation to help "family." "No one is going to look out for all of us; we have to do it for ourselves." "We don't ask for no help from anyone; we just ask for the chance to earn an honest living and the things to do it with." "Looking out for your own" is thus elevated to one of the highest moral virtues.

In Maine coastal towns, a large proportion of the capital assets owned by members of established families—land, houses, family businesses, even island fishing areas—is inherited. These people differ in this respect from other members of the middle class, whose most valuable assets might be a house and a car purchased independently.

Family property is greatly valued, not only for economic reasons, but because of its symbolic worth. Ownership of land locks a person into the past; it confers legitimacy; and it is tangible evidence of ancient roots.

Inheritance of family businesses is especially valued because a good deal of the meaning of life and the respect of others comes from actively participating in the business of one's forefathers and from using and preserving long-held family assets. Even though these small businesses are hardly known outside the local region, within a restricted area they confer prestige. An individual does not have to own land or a business to have such benefit. The fact that someone in the family does so establishes a person's position in the community. For these reasons, people hold onto family homesteads, farms, and land long after their usefulness has passed. At times, these assets are maintained at great financial sacrifice.

People are often very angry when family property is sold, even when the sale is by a family member with a perfect legal right to sell it. The family member who sells a piece of property may be treated with hostility, while the purchaser is often ostracized. If the land is sold to someone outside the community, the purchaser's property rights are enforced with difficulty.

A woman from New Jersey foolishly bought a piece of shorefront land that the former owners, who were lobstermen, had long used as a landing site. They continued using it after she built her cottage. When she objected, they no longer painted their boats on her land, but they let it be known around town that she "went sunbathing naked," and they used her chimney for target practice. Sometimes townspeople act as if a place has not been sold at all. In many towns, houses are known by the names of the first owners—although the houses may have been in the hands of outsiders for decades.

The rules governing inheritance in Maine are complicated, and their execution often causes hard feelings among family members. Two key principles apply.[7] First, a person should have an interest in the land and be willing to sacrifice to maintain it. Second, a value placed on equity and utility lies behind many decisions concerning inheritance. People believe that all family members should have "no more than their share," and that assets should be productive, not held in storage by people who can make no use of them. For this reason, family members who have established themselves in the professions and other businesses, those who have moved away, and women who have husbands to "take care of them" and who no longer use the "family name" often do not receive the same consideration in inheritance decisions as people who reside locally and can make obvious personal use of the asset.

Family members clearly have preference when openings become available in skilled occupations or local businesses. The feeling of responsibility to provide for family members was expressed well by the owner of a large herring stop-seine operation; when asked why he hired only his sons and his sons-in-law, he answered, "It is my responsibility to make sure that these jobs go to the people who are going to feed the members of my family" (i.e., his daughters and grandchildren). Others hired kin because they did not want the family business to "fall into the hands of strangers." Although hiring kin can cause problems, it also has many benefits from the local point of view. Owners of businesses feel that they can trust their kin more and can count on kin to keep secrets about the firm's methods and problems. Kin also can be expected to work longer hours, help out in an emergency, and even forfeit wages on occasion. The number of wives and children who collect no paycheck from such firms is legion. It is standard practice in the fishing industry for wives to do many essential tasks, such as answering the phone, dealing with lawyers and accountants, doing the books, and making deals concerning marketing and maintenance, with no hourly compensation.

The relative-employee knows the job is secure in that he or she is apt to be the last laid off in bad times. Relatives are likely to receive preference in jobs demanding special training or skills. In addition, a relative who is a longtime employee can often arrange to inherit the firm, or at least become a partner in it, far more easily than an employee from another family. Something more subtle is involved as well: kin who work for family firms clearly feel a sense of pride in being part of something that bears their name. They are contributing to a family heritage.

As a result of this strong preference for hiring kin, almost all businesses (stores, carpentry shops, gas stations, restaurants, fishing boats, and others) are manned by a core of relatives. In some firms all of the ten to fifteen employees are close family members. A firm rarely hires more than four or five people who have no kinship ties at all. Of the seventy-nine firms in one town, 74 percent had at least one employee who was closely related to the owner of the firm. This preference leads to concentrations of kin in the same occupation, with the result that certain family names are associated with certain activities.

Like businesspeople anywhere else, people in these towns borrow from banks much of the capital for long-term investment projects. However, kin ties are frequently used to gain access to large amounts of capital. People generally borrow from members of their nuclear household or other close family members. Many loans apparently call for no interest or no contract. In some cases the loan is not expected to be repaid. Such loans have all the earmarks of a patrimony.

Relatives outside the close range of kinship feel no obligation to lend money and require collateral and formal agreements if any sizable amounts are involved. In such cases, interest is charged, since the object of making the loan is not only to help a relative but to make money.

A very large percentage of young lobstermen are aided in establishing themselves in business by loans from parents and other close relatives. Rod Forsgren, a professor of business administration who is an amateur lobster fisherman and an acute observer of the fishing scene on the island where he maintains a summer home, believes that most young fishermen "receive substantial help from their parents or other relatives. . . . The costs of going into business are so high today and returns are so low that it is very difficult for a youngster to start a small operation and gradually expand his business" (personal communication 1986).[8] But people feel ambivalence about obtaining large amounts of cash from kinsmen. They recognize that if such loans or partnerships can be advantageous, they can also be very dangerous and lead to serious rifts.

For businesspeople in every industry, much of the most valuable information comes from others in the same industry in the same area. In Maine coastal communities, kin often have a great deal of valuable information for each other because so many of them are working at the same occupation.

Many different kinds of information are passed between people, particularly kin in the same industry: information on reliability of employees, on sources of credit and credit risks, and on new business practices and innovations. Kinfolk also pass along business to one another and often cooperate in lobbying local and state officials for changes in the legal environment favorable to their industry.

The exact way that kinship ties are used differs substantially from industry to industry. Kin in the Maine fishing industry often swap information about concentrations of fish, markets, fishing practices, and technical innovations. Novices in the industry may obtain training and skills by working on the boats of older kin. Given the importance of the information that kin exchange, having many relatives in the industry is a distinct advantage.

The number of kinsmen that a man has in fishing is undoubtedly linked to success. In our 1978 study of Maine fishing captains, 62 percent of the "highline" (outstanding) fishermen in our sample of 122 reported they had "a lot of kinsmen" in their home ports, while only 37 percent of the "dub" (poor) fishermen made this claim.

One of the most vital resources reserved for local people is access to lobster-fishing areas. Lobster-fishing rights along the entire Maine coast are, for all practical purposes, owned by local fishing groups. Territoriality in the lobster industry will be discussed in more detail in the next chapter, but it should be noted here that in most harbors it is much easier for people from established families to gain entry into harbor gangs.

Political success in small Maine towns requires an actual power base and a legitimate right to authority. Both power and legitimacy are obtained through the manipulation of kin ties. The maneuvers for gaining political support, however, are vastly different from the strategies used to clothe oneself in legitimacy. Real power in the form of votes is obtained through private exchanges with kin, friends, and acquaintances. One of the primary ways to gain legitimacy is through a public and symbolic manipulation of genealogical links to the past.

According to Maine law, any person over twenty-one years old has a right to run for local political office. In most small coastal towns, however, if a candidate does not come from an established family or lineage, he or she might as well not bother to run. In a recent election for selectman in one of the towns under study, a personable,

college-educated man was soundly defeated by a man whose family
had lived in town for generations. The newcomer never stood a
chance. As one elderly woman put it, "How could he do the job? He
has only been here for seven years." An urban sophisticate might
find it quaint that political jobs are reserved for "established people."
What surprises local people is that a person living in the town for
less than a decade would "have the brass" to run for high office.

Eligibility to run for office in such towns is ordinarily based on a
person's history, experience, and, most important, genealogy. Normally, when candidates for office advertise their credentials, they
emphasize, not their education or their proposed programs, but their
family's history in the community. The longer and more illustrious
the lineage, the stronger the claims to legitimacy. In the school
board elections in one town, there were nine candidates. In the
newspaper accounts concerning the election, the candidates for the
most part did not directly comment on the several controversial
issues facing the schools; instead they discussed Revolutionary War
heroes, Civil War dead, town founders, famous ship captains, and
events of the seventeenth and eighteenth centuries. The exceptions
to this rule were the newcomers, who were forced to stress such ir-
relevancies as whether they favored abolishing a kindergarten.

Newcomers running for office must use ingenuity. One woman
running for school board had no kin who had lived full time in the
town for at least three hundred years. She was a newcomer in every
sense of the word. She emphasized to the newspaper reporter that
her grandchild would attend the school when her son and his family
moved to town and that one of her relatives was on a ship that sank
in nearby waters in the 1600s on its way from England to Virginia.
She won in an upset. (It must be added, however, that she alone
among the candidates used her own car to transport elderly voters.)

Genealogical linkages to the past give political legitimacy in the
present for several reasons. People who stress their ties with the past
are making a moral statement, emphasizing that they are members
of the core of the community and can be counted on to make political decisions in line with town values and attitudes. They also demonstrate long-term interest and commitment to the town. While

voters have only the word of a newcomer that he or she will not impose "some crazy thing" on the community if elected, the electorate
may look at the record of a candidate with a long genealogical history and determine constancy and predictability, not only in the current generation but also from the activities of ancestors as well. A
vote is exchanged for the promise of maintaining the status quo.
Outsiders have no way of symbolically making such promises. Moreover, community people feel that where political office is concerned,
one must wait one's turn, must "queue up," even if it takes a century or more.

Finally, local people assume that long-term residence is necessary
for competence in office. Knowing everyone and knowing "local
ways" are usually considered more crucial for success in these offices than is any kind of technical skill or experience an "outsider"
might have to offer.

People from established families are not only far more eligible to
run for office; they also have an advantage in getting the votes. Almost every person from these families has a widespread network of
kin, whose votes alone may propel the candidate into office. This
factor is obviously not decisive when opposing candidates are both
from established families, but it plays a significant role where one
candidate has a generous network of kin with greater genealogical
roots in the community. Candidates, however, cannot take the votes
of their kin for granted. Serious aspirants make a habit of calling
their relatives to ask for their votes as they would any other prospec-
tive voter. In one town almost all important town officers since 1840
were from families whose names had appeared on the tax rolls for at
least fifty years.

Nevertheless, newcomers are increasingly finding their way to political office in Maine coastal towns. Educated retirees, especially,
bring well-honed verbal skills to the arena, long experience with bureaucracy, a concern for "good government," and a good deal of lei-
sure time with which to pursue office. Many of these newcomer
officeholders advocate badly needed programs and reforms. Their
efforts are often met with hostility, and many people from established families consider them to be dangerous meddlers. Still, immi-

gration is adding to the power base of the newcomers. In the future, many more outsiders will elect one another to public office.

Entry into Communities

Members of established families have a clear edge on other people in the towns. Not only are they eligible to run for political office; their large kin network will deliver the votes. Not only do they feel that they should have the land; they actually have a lot of it. Not only do they feel an obligation to "look out for their own"; they really give the jobs and training to close kin. As a result, it is axiomatic in these towns that a successful person is one from an old, established family, and members of such old families will be successful. Here there is virtue of a most practical kind in staying in the same place for generations. As one fisherman phrased it: "The secret of success around here is to have an old family and a big boat." One is merely the expression of the other.

The relationship between longevity and economic and political success has some odd twists. If a group of kin is successful in business, people simply assume that the family has been around for a long while. Sometimes this simply is not true. In one town, two very successful businesses are owned by sets of kin assumed to have been in the area for a long time. In fact, both came around the turn of the century. On the other hand, old established families whose members have not done well are considered anomalous. In these cases, people feel that something needs to be explained.

Some immigrants to Maine coastal towns explain their alienation in terms of not having been born in the town. A former New Jerseyite said, "There is a virtue in sitting in the same place for two hundred years." While such statements are often made in jest, kinship and community are strongly linked. Without kinship ties, it is difficult for a person to be considered anything but an outsider. More than mere ancestry is involved however.

Membership in the community requires two commitments. The first is a moral commitment: people are members of the community when they and their kin accept the local value system and the yardstick by which behavior is judged. But membership in a community is not solely a matter of behaving in an approved manner. *Acceptance* of the standard of conduct—not how well an individual lives up to its precepts—is critical in defining a member of the community. The second criterion for membership is long-term residence and interaction with local people. A person is expected to interact a good deal within the town but also is expected not to know too many outsiders.

People from all established families are automatically members of the community. They have lived in the town for generations; they are involved in a variety of social activities; and their acceptance of the community's values has been tested through time. It does not make any difference whether the family has a good or a bad reputation. The fact of having a reputation is critical. A person from one of these kin groupings is a known quantity—for better or for worse—in the eyes of the community. He or she is not like an outsider whose actions are unpredictable. Referring to tourists, one fisherman said: "Christ, you never know what they are going to do." Clearly, knowing what to expect—even if it is bad—is very important.

Every coastal town has a number of summer people whose families have owned cottages for generations. Some of these folk have essentially the same values as local people. Why are they not considered community members? The basic problem apparently is that these people are not able to interact with long-term residents frequently enough. They cannot attend meetings and gatherings most of the year and are not part of a set of kin who interact within a communal framework. Even if they have the right values, this is not known because there is no chance to test them. In actuality, most summer people neither have the right values nor do they interact. While they are physically present in the town, they are black holes in the social universe.

Given that membership in these Maine communities is tied up with membership in long-established families, such communities would seem to be hermetically sealed against all outsiders, who cannot change their birthplace and cannot easily marry into an old family, especially since members of kin lines tend to intermarry. Nonetheless, the boundaries around Maine communities are relatively permeable. Any town contains a number of people in the process of being accepted. How they gain entry and the nature of the boundaries they must cross deserve careful analysis.

Entry into these communities is slow. A newcomer to a small Maine town cannot gain entry immediately, though certain steps can be taken. Although a newcomer can never achieve the same degree of acceptance that a member of an established family inherits, his or her children or grandchildren will have much more success.

While the residents of these towns use polarized categories such as "insider" or "outsider," our analysis suggests that there are many intermediate stages between complete strangers and members of the core community. An individual entering the community moves along a continuum rather than making a quantum leap to full-fledged community member. This continuum has five statuses: visitor, resident, person establishing community ties, member of the moral community, and member of the core or genealogical community.[9]

Visitors, of course, visit the town briefly or live there only seasonally. Most people who live in summer cottages are almost as much outsiders as the casual visitor. They do not know anyone and may be completely unknown by the community itself. Residents live in the town year round but interact very little.

People who move into town and take steps to increase community ties are in the next category. Three kinds of activities greatly increase the number of ties possible: (1) having "a family" (i.e., a nuclear family), which allows them to become known at school and gives their children access to peer-group ties; (2) having a job in town; and (3) participating actively in one or more of the many clubs, associations, political organizations, or churches. Some summer people whose families have owned cottages in town for decades and who take pains to join many organizations fit in this category.

Membership in the moral community occurs when a person has consistently exhibited many of the values previously described and interacts intensively over a long period. Last, membership in the core community is held only by members of long-established families. The core community has some marginal members, individuals who were born into established families but have chosen to live on the margin or else are not completely acceptable.

The road to community membership begins with a move into the town. None of the other steps is possible unless a person is a full-time resident. Then the resident must demonstrate concern for the town; finally the person must conform to the accepted values to become a member of the moral community.

Oldtimers in small Maine towns think they know exactly how newcomers can achieve community membership. When we asked one woman, "What should I do if I want to become part of this community?" we got a primer of activities: I must move into the area, live on the main road, be married (preferably with children), get a job in or around the town, join local organizations, be involved in community affairs, and avoid "rocking the boat" by injecting alien attitudes into the community.

A move into the area is synonymous with residence; marriage, a local job, membership in organizations and participation in community affairs all increase network ties. The admonition not to rock the boat is a comment about moral commitment. It recognizes that if a newcomer cannot agree with all of the local ideology, he or she should not advertise the fact. The advice about living on the main road is also a moral statement: only "hippies" live in the woods, after all.

This woman stated that no visitor could ever become a true part of "us," the inner core; she was fully aware that membership in the core community could be attained only by birth. This college-educated woman had experienced her own difficulties in accepting all aspects of the local outlook. She expressed doubt that any educated newcomer could accept enough of the value system to enter the moral community.

The length of time it takes to go from outsider to core community member varies considerably. A person who moves into the town immediately becomes a resident and can join enough local clubs, political groups, and other organizations to have a large number of ties in two to five years. If the person can create enough ties in a short time, he or she can demonstrate proper values fairly quickly. A person could conceivably move from visitor to member of the moral community within half a decade, but that person can never move into the core community. Even a newcomer marrying into the core community does not become part of it, although his or her children will be—particularly if they stay in town and emphasize the right genealogical ties.

Exit from these communities is relatively easy and happens all the time. A person merely has to move out of the region to be forgotten by most inhabitants within a few years. However, people can lose rights even if they stay in town. People from established families who adopt values at odds with those defining the moral community can have trouble. For this reason higher education is considered dangerous. One schoolteacher from a very old family said that she was almost an outcast because she supported art classes and kindergarten, which local opinion had branded ridiculous. She took other unpopular stands, demonstrating her lack of commitment to the proper values.

People can also lose some of the rights of full-fledged members by ceasing to interact. Several members of established families mentioned cousins, uncles, and others who were physically present in the town but who "stuck to themselves" for one reason or another, or were so "odd" that others would not interact with them.

Ordinarily, a member of the core community who moves away from town can reclaim full rights upon return. Many people who have served in the military for twenty years or worked out of town for decades find it relatively easy, on their return, to pick up where they left off, though there are exceptions to this rule. If the absence lasts too long, people lose certain rights, particularly if they have not attended school in the town.

People who have moved into coastal Maine towns react to being outside the community in a variety of ways. Middle-class individuals often move only part way along the continuum and are content to stay there. They have many friends and are active in a variety of social groups. Evidently they do not want to take on the values that would make them members of the moral community; in fact, their horizons are such that the community cannot be the focal point of their lives. Their close friends, who are apt to be professional and business people, share this category. They live in town but appreciate the partial anonymity that goes with marginal acceptance.

Lower-middle-class immigrants often seem to feel more strain.

Many would like to join the core community but cannot, by virtue of birth. Though they may have lived in the town for decades, share the values, and have many friends and acquaintances, they are marginal in many respects. Their sense of dissatisfaction sometimes finds voice. One popular fisherman, who had lived in his town for close to forty years, said, "Regardless of what I do or how much I achieve, I can never be fully accepted in this town. Some people are always going to look down on me—I was born in Massachusetts. They were born here. That's all that counts."

CHAPTER 3

Harbor Gangs

While lobstermen themselves often subscribe to the stereotype of the independent man-at-sea, they are in fact part of a complicated social network. The industry has rules that all men are expected to obey, its own standards of conduct, and its own mythology. To succeed in lobstering a man not only must have certain technical skills and work hard, but also must be able to operate in a particular social milieu.

Beyond the kinship group, the most important people in a lobster fisherman's life are the men who fish from the same harbor. Such social groupings, while they are recognized by everyone in the lobster-fishing industry, have no universally accepted name. People refer to the "Monhegan boys," or the "Friendship fishermen," or the "Port Clyde gang." Sometimes men refer to those in their own harbor as "the men I fish with." I have called these groups "harbor gangs," although this term is only rarely used by the fishermen themselves (Acheson 1972).

Membership in a harbor gang strongly influences many aspects of a lobster fisherman's career. Most importantly, it controls entry into the industry. To go lobster fishing, a man must first become a member of a harbor gang. Once he has gained admission, he can go fishing only in the territory "owned" communally by members of that gang.

Fishermen who place their traps in the territory of another gang can expect swift retribution, normally the purposeful destruction of their gear. Although these territories and the gangs that own them are completely unrecognized by the state, they are a long-standing reality. Fishermen identify with a particular harbor gang and are identifed as members of it. Members of harbor gangs obtain a great deal of valuable information from one another on fishing locations and innovations. They also assist one another in times of emergency at sea. If a motor breaks down or someone runs out of gas, other members of the gang are called for a tow. This is one of the reasons that people in a harbor gang keep their radios on the same channel.

Harbor gangs are also reference groups. Members measure themselves against one another in determining success and skill. A lobster fisherman competes with members of his own gang, and it is these men whose opinions count. A man is a good fisherman or a bad fisherman primarily in comparison with others in the local lobster fishery. The men of one harbor gang do not compare themselves with the men in others; they simply do not know many people in other gangs. To these men it is almost inconceivable that they should compare themselves with captains of scallopers or draggers or seiners, even though those captains might live in the same town or even next door. Men in other fishing industries are playing very different games with very different standards.

Lobster fishermen in the same harbor gang ordinarily have long-term, multistrand ties with one another. Almost all live in the town where the harbor is located. Many are members of long-established families and share kinship ties as well. The men of the same generation have grown up together, and members of their families have known one another and intermarried for generations.

Every member of a harbor gang knows every other member by sight and reputation, regardless of their degree of interaction. In the smaller harbor gangs, with perhaps ten or a dozen fishermen, all of them might interact with all others several times a week. In the larger gangs, which include more than a hundred men, members might go weeks without seeing some of the other members.

Within any harbor gang, cliques and friendships form among individuals fishing for the same dealer or from the same cooperative dock. In many harbors, there may be as many cliques of fishermen as there are dealers or cooperatives. Men fishing from the same dock talk and joke together before leaving for the day's work. Some dealers provide a place, which serves as a clubhouse, for their fishermen to sit, talk, and drink coffee.

The interaction between men of the same gang continues at sea. Once or twice a day, between pulling traps, lobster fishermen stop their boats out on the water to talk to friends. Almost all lobster fishermen have citizen's band radios on board, and many converse with others in the same harbor gang. They rarely contact men from neighboring harbors, and men from different harbors customarily use different channels. Even ashore, interaction between lobster fishermen in the same harbor is very intense. In one community studied, of 133 lobster fishermen (owners and sternmen) who were asked to name their "best friends," 87 named another lobster fisherman in the same harbor gang.[1]

The amount of interaction among fishermen varies considerably. Some fishermen spend hours each day hanging around the wharfs, visiting fish houses and one another's homes, and chattering to one another on the CB radio at sea. Others remain quite solitary. They may come down to the dock in the morning, get gas and bait, and leave for a day's fishing without many words to anyone. During the day, such men may use their radios only once or twice. Some of these men are considered marginal to the harbor gang; others are very popular and are considered to be important members. I know one skilled fisherman, highly esteemed by the men with whom he fishes, who listens to the AM radio—not the CB or VHF radio—whenever he is pulling traps. Since he has his own dock and lobster car, he goes to the dealer's dock once in several days, yet he is widely considered the "finest kind" of fisherman around.

Occasionally all of the fishermen from a harbor gang may meet. The fishermen on Monhegan are reputed to meet in the house of one of the gang leaders in December or early January to decide on trap day, the day when they will begin fishing again. I have also heard that two small harbor gangs held meetings to decide on a common defense against an encroachment on their fishing territory. But these cases are exceptions. In the few harbors where there are cooperatives, meetings may involve most of the gang members but rarely include all, since a few men always choose to sell their lobsters elsewhere.

Within each gang, small cliques of friends and relatives form. These individuals help one another with tasks requiring cooperative effort, such as launching or hauling up a boat or a float, or putting an engine in a boat. If one man becomes ill, others in the clique usually pull his traps and give him the proceeds until he recovers. Clique members also lend one another tools and sometimes build traps or paint buoys together. Close ties often develop. During these work stints the men are constantly gossiping, joking, and talking with other fishermen who might visit. During or after these sessions, men play cards, drink a few beers or something with more force, and perhaps cook steaks. In many instances, their wives get to be good friends as well, so that two or more couples occasionally go out to eat or dance, and in a few instances even take vacations together.

Lobstermen have little or no contact with their counterparts in other harbors, even harbors only a few miles distant. It is quite common to meet fishermen who have not visited harbors within ten miles of their home port for years. The geography of the Maine coast, with its long peninsulas, does not facilitate contact, nor does the competition between harbor gangs for fishing territory.

Members of each harbor gang are believed to have certain traits, attitudes, or techniques that mark them as a little different from those of other gangs. Many of the stereotypes are very negative. The men of one harbor gang continually refer to the men from another town as "cunners" (small fish) and say that they are "strange." The men from Monhegan supposedly "like to play fisherman for the tourists. They all call themselves captain, you know. The goddamned fools will wear boots and slicker in the store right in the middle of a sunny summer day so people will know who they are." Those from another island are said to be bunch of rowdies, "burnt-out cases from the Vietnam War. Booze, dope, and girl swapping are their hobbies." The fishermen from Friendship are known as a "church-going bunch. Real fundamentalist, you know." Somehow, even religious conviction is made to sound vaguely sinister.

There is often a shred of truth in the statements. Some individuals in each harbor do act like "outlaws" or "swap girlfriends" or "smoke pot." They are not, however, singled out but are used to stereotype whole gangs, including men who certainly bear none of these traits. The quirks are seized upon, while the positive traits and highly successful fishermen are forgotten. The negative images stem largely from the competition between gangs for lobster-fishing territory. If a man has not had trouble personally with members of adjacent harbors, he has a brother, uncle, or friend who has.

The Social Hierarchy

In any fishery, a hierarchy ranks men from "highliners," who catch a lot of fish and have high incomes, to "dubs," poor fishermen with low returns. The same is true in the lobster fishery. This skill-and-income hierarchy is the most important feature of the social structure of any harbor gang and manifests itself in several different spheres. The reference group of fisherman—the men he compares himself with—consists of those in his own harbor gang. His standing in the region as a whole and his income in comparison with men in other fishing industries are largely irrelevant.

Being known as a highliner can affect the way a person is treated throughout life. Even very old and retired fishermen are treated with deference if they were once "big fish killers." In time, such men can become folk heroes in coastal fishing communities, and their stories are told for generations. Their reputations are enhanced by nice houses, good trucks, large and well-equipped boats, and other objects valued in the community. Many of these possessions have both symbolic and practical value, as capital equipment useful for continued fishing success.

The prestige enjoyed by highline fishermen is especially great if they adhere to other valued community norms and goals. For this reason, the status of older highline fishermen from old families who are "good family men" and "level-headed fishermen" is high. Fishing success can compensate for a good many other sins. A foul-mouthed boor, a drunk, or a vicious gossip does not seem so bad if it can be added "but he is a good fisherman." Among lobster fishermen, highliners are known in adjacent harbors as well. Save for highliners, lobstermen typically cannot name many fishermen in harbors even ten miles away.

Dubs have low prestige and are accorded little deference. In the lobster fishery, most of the dub fishermen are young and inexperienced individuals who are expected to become good fishermen in time. But every harbor also has lobstermen who just cannot seem to "catch fish" regardless of what they do. Often their lack of success is explained in terms of inherited traits: "He just don't have a nose for fish; his father was the same way. You could give them the best traps in the world and the finest bait and they would put them where there never had been any lobsters." At other times, lack of success is explained by other traits and habits: laziness, alcoholism, drugs, stupidity. Since the lack of fishing success results in low incomes, such fishermen often live in very poorly maintained houses, drive old automobiles, and invariably have small old boats and poor fishing gear. Their lack of success is exposed for all to see. The prestige accorded them is especially low if they also conspicuously violate essential norms. Marital problems, problems with the law, odd personal mannerisms, being known as a "goddamned hippie," or coming from "out of state" can be the final nails in the coffin.

Such men may be ridiculed openly and become the butt of vicious jokes. One old man who "never had been a good fisherman" periodically has his dory filled with rotten bait, and his outhouse catches fire on occasion. Other men become the subject of apocryphal stories. One local fisherman, noted for his slack jaw, vacant expression, lack of fishing success, and periodic employment of his daughter (with whom some suspect he is having an incestuous relationship) as a sternman, is a case in point. "He fucks her every time they get a lobster. One time last summer she got it twice before lunch." Other stories about dubs reflect both ridicule and humor, touched with a bit of awe. In one harbor a poor fisherman with long hair who lives on a local island with his girlfriend is famous for both his lack of navigating ability and his capacity to drink immense quantities of liquor on board. He has reputedly found his way home on several foggy nights by spinning a liquor bottle he has just emptied and then going in the direction to which it points. By all reports, the tech-

nique works well for him. The fishermen in both these stories are
almost certainly being slandered by gossips with more regard for a
good story than the truth, but such tales underline the calumny to
which poor fishermen can be subjected, especially if fishing inept-
itude is compounded by violation of other expectations.[2]

In all fisheries, no one wants to be tagged a dub, and there is great
competition to be a good fisherman and a highliner. To some men,
fishing is a game. One very successful lobster fisherman said, "We
just go out in the morning, and it is kind of fun to see who gets the
most by nightfall. It's a kind of sport. It just adds a little spice to
the day."

Competition can be particularly fierce among highliners—in fact,
it may become a primary goal. For these men, fishing is not just
a way to make a living. They strive to beat the others and avoid
being beaten by them. The competition within a harbor gang sometimes becomes very serious, even vicious. Many poor fishermen are
thought, with some justification, to steal lobsters from other men's
traps. Others lie to cover up their lack of success. Many are very secretive about catches and numbers of traps. It is also common for
fishermen to try to avoid giving out too much information while re-
vealing enough about their success to avoid being thought a dub.
Even highliners feel the pressure. On one island, two brothers, highliners, are known to be very spiteful to younger fishermen whose
catches threaten to overtake their own. Two other very good lobster
fishermen in another harbor, who had been friends for years, are no
longer on speaking terms after one caught the other taking lobsters
out of his traps and disturbing his gear. The victim sadly said that
the former friend "just couldn't stand to get beat. He knew I was getting more than he was and he couldn't take it. He was taking a few
of my lobsters every time he went out pulling, just to keep even
with me."

There is, of course, nothing particularly surprising about the com-
petitiveness. Like other American males, lobster fishermen set great
store on technical competence and monetary success. But competition causes men to do things they would not otherwise consider. As
one fisherman put it: "They drive each other something awful." In
some lobstering harbors, men feel pride in being the first one out in

the morning and the last one in at night. They note who goes fishing (and who does not) and for how many hours. Whether men go out in marginal weather often depends on the actions of others. I have watched fishermen decide whether to go fishing when it was raining and blowing outside the harbor. As long as no one made a move to go fishing, all would stay on the dock. But the instant one man set out, others followed. Unhappy and swearing, they would go, driven by their unwillingness to let another get ahead. On one cold day when the wind was blowing so hard that traps had to be held on the rail of the boat, everyone went fishing. After we had been out many hours, I was told, "You can blame that goddamned [highliner]. If he hadn't gone out, we would be sitting up at Moody's Diner drinking hot coffee and watching the girls." This remark was a joke, but the highliner really was the cause of our predicament.

Competition underlies another phenomenon: the marked escalation in the number of lobster traps during the past forty years. This escalation first came about in every harbor as one or two men began to build more traps to obtain a larger portion of the available lobsters, and others increased their own traps to keep up. The results are huge numbers of traps. Men who would have had 150 traps thirty years ago might have 500 today. This escalation makes no sense from an economic point of view. Only a fixed number of lobsters molt to legal size in a given area, and almost all are caught within the year. Increasing the number of traps will not result in a larger total of lobsters caught and has certainly added to the costs of gas, bait, and traps. Although most lobster fishermen understand this situation, they have steadily added more traps to keep up with the competition.

Maine lobster fishermen feel ambivalent toward men who catch many lobsters. A great deal of prestige accrues to these highliners, yet the respect may not completely counter the feeling that their success is at the expense of others. Men who fish huge "gangs" of traps or who fish in bad weather are often considered to be taking advantage of others. These "pigs" or "hogs" can stir up a good deal of antagonism. The feeling against such a man may run particularly high if he is a braggart and his high income is thought to be due more to effort and capital equipment than to skill. Several reasons account for this reaction against "success." Lobstering territories are considered the property of all the men in a particular harbor gang, and there is a strong feeling that all members should have equal access to the resource. Fishermen and lobster biologists are convinced that a fixed number of legal-size lobsters inhabit any given area. If one man takes them, another cannot. In addition, men who fish very large numbers of traps or brag about their success raise the level of competition in a gang, sometimes to an uncomfortable degree. The feelings against these men are closely akin to the sentiment against "rate busters" in a factory setting, for many of the same reasons.

People also believe that many fishermen who fish large numbers of traps and work especially hard are compensating for lack of skill. Their average or even above-average incomes do not make them "good fishermen." Sometimes the reaction to them borders on contempt. One fisherman, who was known to work sixteen hours a day and who fished a huge gang of traps, finally saved enough money to build a very expensive waterfront house of the type that usually only wealthy retirees can afford. Several people admired the house but noted that the man was not really a good fisherman. One said, "The only thing that saves ——— from being a dub is a thousand traps and a strong back."

In short, the various rules defining success among lobstermen conflict to some degree. A man is motivated to compete for a high income and to demonstrate his success by conspicuously consuming that income according to the dictates of American society. Too much success, or success earned the wrong way, however, can generate envy, hostility, and gossip. Most fishermen attempt to escape from this double bind by being secretive about the number of their traps, their catches, and their incomes.

The ideal man comes into view. He is a skilled fisherman who lets it be known in quiet ways that he earns a high income by working a small or moderate number of traps. He is an easygoing, helpful fellow who takes only his fair share of the lobsters and does not escalate the level of competition. His prestige increases with age, but even a young man of this type is greatly admired and respected in a coastal community. Very few fishermen live up to this ideal completely. Men who have high incomes work hard and rarely have a small number of traps. Inevitably, they take more lobsters than average, and their high incomes excite some envy. But the ideal is instructive, nevertheless.

The Flow of Information

The hierarchy of fishermen in each harbor gang strongly influences the access to information and the information flow in the gang. Information about catches, gear, and concentrations of lobsters is very valuable. If a man locates a concentration of lobsters, he can fish in the same spot for a period of days or even weeks if the spot is not known to others. As a result, secrecy is the rule. One coastal resident said, "They are the goddamnedest bunch of liars you have ever seen. They never admit when they are into the lobsters. You would think they were all eligible for food stamps." Fishermen tend not to divulge all they know unless the information they obtain in exchange is worth at least as much as what they are giving. In general, then, fishermen can get accurate information only from those of approximately equal levels of skill. Highline fishermen are most likely to exchange information with other highly skilled men. Intermediate-level fishermen can get a good deal of worthwhile information from highliners, but cannot give much back. Intermediates are unlikely to give accurate information to low-skilled fishermen; as a result, they too exchange information primarily with other men in the intermediate skill range. Dubs likewise are stuck talking to other dubs. No fishermen of higher levels of skill can get much from talking to dubs except material for jokes.

There are two exceptions to his rule. Very close relatives exchange accurate information regardless of skill level. Fathers, uncles, and grandfathers feel obligated to help sons, nephews, and grandsons. In addition, men who wish to become leaders of harbor gangs often advise young and sometimes less-skilled fisherman in an attempt to gain their loyalty. Since such leaders are apt to have a good many ties, they are likely to be good sources of information.

Despite fishermen's attempts to keep valued information to themselves, enough highliners give information to men of other skill lev-

els so that fishing secrets are rarely kept for long. As one highline
fisherman expressed it, "All you have to do is tell one of those dub
kids something once and in two weeks it is all over the country."
Thus, information generally flows from the top of the hierarchy to
the bottom.

The flow of information between harbor gangs is usually relatively small, because of enmity and the lack of interaction. Highline
fishermen, however, are an exception. Vitally interested in the industry, they make an effort to maintain contact with others who are
doing things of signficance in the universe of lobster fishing. Many
highliners go out of their way to initiate and maintain ties with
highline fishermen in nearby communities to exchange information
and ideas. These links serve as indirect conduits between harbor
gangs. Close friendships result sometimes. Three highline fishermen from different harbors, whom I know well, have become so
friendly that they and their wives go out to restaurants together and
even take vacations together. The favorite topic of conversation between the men is, of course, fishing.

Leadership

Every harbor gang has at least one man who is recognized as a leader,
sometimes called a "king" or "kingpin," or in aggregate the "bunch
that runs things." Leaders in other harbors have no name denoting
their status, although everyone knows who they are. In all harbors,
leaders are treated with deference. They tend to serve as spokesmen
for the harbor gang to outsiders and officials of all kinds. They are
frequently elected officers of local fishermen's cooperatives, or they
may hold town offices. Their advice is sought by other fishermen on
a variety of subjects and topics. Leaders are called in to help settle
disputes between members of the gang; they are often asked to generate rules or policies to avoid conflict; they impose sanctions against
members of the gang for violations; they often have a voice in deciding who will be allowed to join the gang and who will not. When the
occasion arises, they are instrumental in organizing the defense of
the gang's lobster-fishing territory.

All leaders are successful fishermen. Technical competence and economic success are valued so highly that a poor fisherman is never chosen as a leader, regardless of his other qualities. The power of leaders and their ability to solve problems depend very much on the following they can muster in the harbor gang, which in turn depends on the assets at their disposal, both tangible and moral. Powerful leaders generally are in a position to do favors for others but need not accept favors. Besides being successful fishermen, they are usually middle-aged or older. They almost invariably come from established families and usually have a large number of kinsmen who might become allies. In any large harbor, many men may possess these traits but only a few actually use them strategically to achieve leadership. Others have the mantle of leadership thrust on them, although they probably subtly encourage their own selection.

Styles of leadership vary considerably. One type of leader is the highly autocratic man who bullies younger or weaker men in the harbor gang. On the other end of the spectrum are the leaders who conform somewhat to the ideal of the "good fisherman." These men are likely to have wide circles of friends and can successfully demonstrate their fishing skills without raising antagonism. Harbor gangs commonly have leaders of both types, and some are between the two extremes.

How leadership in harbor gangs is achieved, along with its various functions, is best conveyed by an example. In one isolated community with about 250 permanent residents, the major industry is lobster fishing. In 1980 there were some thirty lobster fishermen, virtually all of whom sold their catches to the cooperative. The leaders of two large, established families in town are also the leaders of the local harbor gang. One of these men, a fifty-five-year-old fisherman, is called the king of the gang; his father was king before him. He is the acknowledged leader among his four sons and other close kinsmen, and eight other men are known to be his followers as well.

The king's style of power is authoritarian. He has the capacity to bully other fishermen or the cooperative manager and to discipline them for real or imagined violations of norms. Many times the king himself does not impose discipline openly but uses some of his followers as messengers, although members of the harbor gang always know where the message originated. The king, his family, and his followers run the local lobster cooperative, having monopolized all of its offices since its founding, and make all decisions concerning capital improvements, dividends, salaries of employees, and membership. They are also instrumental in maintaining the gang's lobster-fishing territory. The king himself might not apply sanctions against interlopers but organizes and reinforces those who do. The king and his supporters also have the power to allocate fishing locations. The forty good fishing spots in the gang's territory are controlled by various cliques. The best locations are reserved for members of the king's family or the other established family. At times, the king uses his influence to "open up" one or more good fishing spots to a relative newcomer.

The king's power comes from several sources. He and the other men in his family are very good fishermen; his wealth has steadily increased. He is also a perceptive individual who is good at playing off people against one another. Most important, however, is the king's ability to build a large following. He constantly works to attach others to him, using several techniques: he forces other fishermen into transactions with him and continually does them favors. He and his family own the equipment to move boats and the spray guns to remove barnacles, and they charge other fishermen only a nominal fee for use of this equipment. He and his sons help other fishermen haul up their boats and lend tools, gear, and assistance on many other occasions. He is also constantly handing out small gifts. One fisherman in town pointed out that if a person were either to reject the king's help or to accept it and pay him back completely, the king could become hostile. Another said, "He always has to be the big shot and be giving everyone something all the time. It's bad when you got to take something from someone. They always use it against you."

Gang members also recognize, however, that the king, his sons, and his followers have taken primary responsibility for two institutions that benefit all the fishermen in the gang: the cooperative and territorial defense. That the cooperative has made money is due in no small part to the leadership of the king and the hard work of his followers. Their defense of the gang's fishing territory is known to be effective, if brutal. In the words of one fisherman, "They ain't always popular, but they are hard workers and have done a lot of the dirty work."

Many followers are attracted to the king by his very conservative ideology. Any conversation with him is likely to lead to discussions or long monologues on such topics such as blacks, the federal and state governments, hippies, welfare, Russians, Jews, bureaucrats, Arabs, and Iran. It is fair to say that the king is against them all. The government is the favorite topic. Among major themes that keep cropping up in his conversations are the waste of tax money, excessive governmental control over the lives of private citizens, the incompetency of government employees, and the waste and immorality of social programs. These ideas are pressed on others, who are expected to agree; arguing against them is considered very bad form. To some of the king's admirers, his political opinions are among his most attractive features, and they sit with him for hours discussing such matters. The fact that many of these same people will accept any kind of government subsidy available is somehow beside the point.

It is easy to conclude that people like the king recall a time of greater individual freedom and are threatened by social and economic changes. This conclusion, however, misses the essential point. When the king expresses such ideas, he is advertising his adherence to some of the highest moral precepts in the culture; when he presses them on other people, he is deliberately manipulating these critical symbols with political advantage in mind. It is a very effective ploy if we can judge by the "moral following" (Bailey 1969: 42ff.) it has produced.

The other leader in town is the patriarch of the largest family. "Uncle George" is a wise man, well liked by most of the people in the community. In his heyday, he was a very good lobsterman. He is also adept at a couple of sophisticated hobbies, has wide intellectual interests, and has published a number of magazine articles. His political views, along with his manner of speaking, are considerably more moderate than those of the king. To talk to him is to talk to a wise grandfather, who can converse intelligently on virtually any subject. He is incredibly shrewd and knows every idiosyncrasy of his hometown and the folk who live there. Although he usually speaks softly, he can be forceful when the occasion arises. He is one of the very few men who can stand up to the king. Fishermen often come to him when they need to talk things over, and he is inevitably the person to whom they turn when disputes arise. He can be counted on to give good advice and to defuse potentially explosive situations. With these talents he serves the local lobstermen as father confessor, judge, and negotiator. He offers what no one else can provide: protection against the excesses of the king and his gang. He can also lower the level of competition and hostility in a community where interpersonal conflict can reach violent proportions.

Despite the fact that Uncle George has many friends in town and is widely respected and obeyed, he cannot be said to command an organized coalition. His following comes from the many friends and relatives whom he has helped quietly over the years; their support enables Uncle George to negotiate effectively to maintain the peace.

As leaders, the king and Uncle George perform different functions, which are almost mutually exclusive. The king and his gang are forces for action and change. They are movers and managers. They cannot relieve tensions; in fact, they are the cause of a good many of them. While Uncle George, on the other hand, can negotiate disputes because he is rarely involved, he plays little role in managing and maintaining the cooperative or in arranging other matters of general concern.

The king and Uncle George are selected by members of the harbor gang for different purposes. One man explained that when he needs help getting something done, he goes to the king; when he needs help "getting some damage undone," he goes to Uncle George. At times the two men are deliberately played off against each other. The young manager of the cooperative said, "If you disagree with the king, you go to Uncle George." On several occasions George worked some magic for him to overturn the king's decisions. The king and Uncle George are valuable to their followers not only for the jobs they do, but also because one can act as balance to the excesses of the other.

In other harbors, the positions of leadership are also generally assumed by successful fishermen from established families. The kinds of services and gifts they exchange for political loyalty differ from those used by the king. On one island, a leader maintains a phone for general use, and he is always willing to use his large boat to take emergency cases to the hospital. Another provides a dock for his sons and a few "friends." Many leaders are instrumental in organizing territorial defense, and they are the ones who see to it that docks and beaches are kept clear of large numbers of traps and obstructions. Others serve in the unenviable job of harbor master, supervising the placement of moorings and ensuring that harbor passage is unobstructed. Quite a number of leaders are active in the cooperatives or the Maine Lobstermen's Association. Other leaders, like Uncle George, are valuable primarily for their ability to defuse competition and mediate disputes. Like the king, some leaders use a very conservative political ideology to attract followers.

Different circumstances bring different leadership styles to the fore. In one mainland harbor, two older men known to be good fishermen ordinarily have a great deal of influence. However, when trouble brews and the gang's territorial claims are challenged, a tough, loud man in his thirties has on occasion been elevated to "war chief." His virtue is apparently that he can command the loyalty of a group of young fishermen, variously described as "thugs," "wild younguns," and "our side," to do the dirty work needed in defense of the area. In times of peace, the leader of this gang sinks back into obscurity, and his followers become more of a liability than an asset.

Entry into Harbor Gangs

Most fishermen enter a harbor gang in the town where they live, though almost every gang has one or more men who live in other townships. In most cases, these fishermen reside in an inland township that has no harbors of its own. The men who fish off the privately owned islands in Penobscot Bay, however, live in towns such as Rockland, Owls Head, Spruce Head, and Tenants Harbor and make the trip to their fishing grounds every day; in the summer, they may stay in camps on the islands for several days at a time.

Gangs are associated with harbors, not townships. In cases where there are several harbors in a township, each harbor has its own gang. The township of Bristol, for example, has three harbors and three harbor gangs: New Harbor, Pemaquid Harbor, and Round Pond. Each has its own membership and its own lobstering area. Ordinarily a man enters only one harbor gang, but under rare circumstances—when a man moves to an adjacent harbor and enters the gang at his new residence while retaining his old affiliation—he may hold dual membership.

There is no automatic association between harbor gang membership and the place the member sells lobsters. Fishermen usually sell their lobsters to a dealer or cooperative in their gang's harbor, but a small number of harbor gang members sell their catches to dealers or cooperatives in other harbors.

Although most fishermen remain in the same harbor gang throughout their working lives, some do move from harbor to harbor. One man moved away from an island to make it easier for his children to attend high school. Another moved from a small island because his wife could not stand the complete lack of privacy entailed by island living. Ten years later, he moved to another harbor inhabited by only a few good fishermen and he "thought he could do better." Still another moved to avoid a serious conflict. But every time a fisherman moves, he must go through the process of gaining entry to another harbor gang.

Anyone seeking to go lobstering experiences a certain degree of hostility from established fishermen. New fishermen usually have some traps molested for the first few months; a couple of fishermen have laughingly said that this almost amounts to an initiation. Established fishermen understandably do not want to share their lobstering area with still more fishermen. The amount of resistance, however, depends on the personal traits of the person seeking to enter a harbor gang and the area he is attempting to enter. Some entrants are never accepted.

A local boy has relatively little trouble entering a mainland harbor gang if his family members have been long-term residents of the community, if his father or another close relative is established in lobster fishing, and if he is well regarded in the community. His entry into lobster fishing can be especially smooth if he begins fishing from a skiff with a few traps while still in high school and gradually develops into a full-time lobsterman after he graduates. Such a boy in effect inherits a place in his father's gang. Entry in a harbor gang is most difficult for a man from out of state, whose family has no connection with lobster fishing, and who has another income. The reaction against such a person is particularly severe if he begins fishing a large gang of lobster traps and does not have many friends or acquaintances among established members of the harbor gang. Such a man is an outsider and is regarded as having no right to local resources; he also has no allies. Furthermore, because he has other income, he is viewed as taking food out of the mouths of those who have no other way to earn a living. In the eyes of most local people, such a man is a "hog" and can never be accepted into the gang. One New Jersey man in his fifties not only had another income and a large gang of traps but also had plenty of unwanted advice to offer local fishermen. He lasted approximately two weeks in the fishing business. Eventually he was forced to leave town.

Natives of these communities sometimes say that only members of old established families can successfully enter lobstering harbor gangs and that newcomers might as well not attempt to go fishing. But lobstering is not a closed industry. Though residence and membership in established families play a role, not all lobstermen are from fishing families, and many newcomers have entered the industry. Long-term residents do suffer less harassment; however, other matters are clearly more important. Perhaps the most important factor is a willingness to obey local norms regarding lobsters and lobstering gear. A man who acquires the reputation for stealing other men's lobsters or damaging the fishing gear of others in the harbor gang does not last long in the lobster business, regardless of family affiliation or length of residence.

Age at time of entry may be equally important. In one harbor studied, all the fishermen who started fishing as teenagers endured little harassment, regardless of family background. Some were from established families; others were from newcomer families but had grown up in town. One man, whose family has been settled in a coastal community near the mouth of the Kennebec River for more than 250 years, left town with his parents when he was eight years old. When he returned to town at age thirty-three, he tried to go lobster fishing, only to have his fishing gear destroyed repeatedly by fishermen whose families had not been in town half as long as his own. The fact that he was a deputy sheriff as well as a member of a family with long, historic roots made no difference. He believes he would have been accepted had his father, brother, or grandfather been a fisherman at the time he wanted to enter the gang. This may be true. His case further suggests that age at entry and allies in the gang may be more important than membership in a long-established family.

Although having an outside source of income can influence entry, it is apparently not critical. Several men with pensions have managed to become lobster fishermen by employing the proper strategy—establishing ties and allies among members of the harbor gang, entering fishing slowly, and obeying local norms.

Competition within a harbor gang can influence entry. Entry into large, growing mainland gangs is often more difficult than entry into gangs where fishermen have retired or left the industry. For this reason, entry into a gang is eased by buying out a retiring fisherman, a tactic that does not increase the number of vessels in a harbor.

Some newcomers meet considerable opposition before they are accepted in harbor gangs. Others operate so skillfully that they encounter little opposition. One such man moved into a Penobscot Bay town from Massachusetts, began driving the local school bus, and after two years started doing a little lobstering in the summer. A few years later, he purchased a big lobster boat and drove the school bus only as a substitute. In three more years he stopped driving the bus altogether. Another fisherman said, "I knew the second he bought a few traps that we were going to have another lobsterman eventually, and that he didn't plan to stay a bus driver longer than necessary. I should have driven him out of business before he got established. After he had been fishing for several years, he got to be part of the town and there just didn't seem to be anything you could rightly do about it."

Part-time fishermen usually have more difficulty gaining acceptance than those who want to go fishing on a full-time basis, even though full-time fishermen undoubtedly take more lobsters. This hostility stems in part from feelings that part-time fishermen already have an adequate income and do not know the rules of the industry or how to fish. Some novices simply follow more experienced fishermen, with whose gear they are constantly entangling their own. Two crimes are being committed here: taking lobsters that belong to someone else and forcing experienced men to waste time untangling gear. Part-time fishermen are thought to have a cavalier attitude toward other men's traps; many experienced fishermen state that part-timers look into other people's traps and even steal lobsters on occasion. "They don't know how to catch any lobsters," one man told me, "so they are always pulling up our traps to see what we have caught and where we have caught them. If you have caught a lot of lobsters, you won't have so many when they are done." The dislike of part-time fishermen is exacerbated because they cannot have sanctions applied to them except at great risk, since they have very little to lose. According to one fisherman, "The most dangerous man around is the part-timer with a skiff and fifty traps. He can destroy every trap you own overnight. If you cut off all his traps, he still hasn't lost anything and he has another job to boot."

Many of the factors that influence entry into mainland harbor gangs also operate with regard to island gangs, but there are some notable differences. It is much more difficult to gain entrance to island harbor gangs, since fishing rights are tied up with land ownership. Entry into harbor gangs that fish the areas around such privately owned, unoccupied islands as Green Island, Metinic, and Little Green Island is limited to family members who have inherited legal ownership of part of an island. These people automatically have a right to fish the waters off the island regardless of age, income, or popularity. Members of families who own no land on the island have no fishing rights at all. No newcomer can possibly enter such gangs.

In some cases, people purchase land on islands or even whole islands to obtain fishing rights. One man bought an island in the Muscle Ridges channel primarily to gain exclusive fishing rights, but also because it was a good real estate investment. He does not live on the island nor does he use it in any way.

Even if the owner is not using his water territory, his fishing rights remain and may be rented out. Individuals who own whole unoccupied islands rent out water areas to men from nearby mainland harbors. Lobstermen fishing in the Metinic Island area, for example, rent fishing rights from members of two families who are the legal owners of the island. Arrangements vary considerably, but in some cases these family members supply the renter with a boat, a gang of traps, and good fishing grounds. The renter supplies his own bait and gas and gives the island's owners half of the gross receipts as return on capital investment and as rent. Where the renter has his own boat, traps, and equipment, he might pay the owner only ten cents per pound of lobsters caught. These rental rights themselves are inherited; those who rent fishing rights from a particular family are usually descended from previous renters.

On permanently occupied islands, ownership of land by itself is not enough to guarantee fishing rights. A number of summer people have bought cottages on such islands as Matinicus, Monhegan, and Swans Island, but they are not allowed to go fishing in those areas. Fishing rights are guaranteed, however, if land ownership is combined with membership in an established island family. Investigation produced no instances in which people meeting these conditions have been refused entry, although individuals from established families who have not been in continuous residence have been harassed.

Once accepted in a gang, members are almost never ejected. A fisherman from one of the permanently occupied islands has long had the reputation of disturbing others' gear, and some people are quite certain he steals lobsters. Nevertheless, no other island fishermen have seriously attempted to drive him out of business. Their reluctance stems both from the knowledge that he would make such an attempt unpleasant and costly, and from the view that his island-family status gives him the right to fish.

A few "off-islanders" have been able to establish themselves on permanently occupied islands such as Matinicus, Swans Island, Monhegan, Vinalhaven, and the Cranberry Isles. Some of these men come from families that have owned summer houses on the islands for decades. They essentially grew up with island children. Other newcomers have managed to establish themselves by making friends and building allies in the gang before starting to fish. Many worked as sternmen for well-established fishermen and purchased land. As on the mainland, such men find it easier to enter harbor gangs if they build up their operations slowly, scrupulously obey local fishing norms, and do not advertise their success unduly.

Unwillingness to admit new fishermen to the harbor gangs on some of these islands can be explained partially in terms of physical limitations. Matinicus, for example, has room for only thirty-three moorings in the harbor, and they are all occupied (Frank Bowles, personal communication 1978). On another island there are only twenty-five houses and they are all taken. In a few cases, islanders have invited people with large families to take up residence in order to retain state school aid. The fathers of the children usually experience little or no difficulty in going lobster fishing, but an invitation to move to an island is not a guarantee of entry into the harbor gang. During the 1980s, residents of Marshall Island were trying to increase the number of permanent residents by promoting a housing development, which would thus ensure services, but they did not want male immigrants to enter lobstering in large numbers. Trouble loomed, because lobster fishing was the island's only industry.

Many of those who attempt to enter such island groups have been unable to stand scrutiny. While it is difficult to get these individuals to talk about their experiences, some feel the islanders were simply looking for an excuse to reserve the lobsters for themselves. Some were rejected because they were purported to have disturbed someone else's gear, others because they caused "trouble" of some undefined sort. One man was driven from an island, so it appeared, because of his Canadian background; another man's "Ayetalian" mother was held against him.

In general, one can predict whether a man who wants to go lobster fishing will be received by a harbor gang, though surprises do occur. One very experienced fisheman with a large family was asked to move onto an island near his mainland home to help keep the school open. Given the invitation and the fact that his wife was from one of the old island families, one might have predicted that his move would succeed. It did not. He was driven from the island after a conflict with the dealer over bait and several shouting matches with other men; he is currently suing several islanders. In contrast, two University of Maine professors have established themselves as part-time lobster fishermen on islands east of Penobscot Bay, where they own summer cottages. One said, "I couldn't have gone fishing in a big way the first year we bought the camp [summer cottage], but once I got to know the local fishermen, I had no difficulty."

Fishing rights in mainland harbors are usufructuary to a large extent. If a person moves away and stops fishing, his claim to fishing rights becomes progressively weaker. His children will have a more difficult time entering fishing than they would if he were an active member of the harbor gang. Under no circumstances can such a person's fishing rights be inherited by other family members. If he stays away from the town and from fishing for a few years, he himself might have difficulties rejoining his gang. On islands, the sense of ownership is far stronger and more permanent. There, inheritance of legal rights to a piece of land automatically carries with it rights to fish in the island's lobster-fishing area, in the view of those in the local culture if not in the eyes of the law. Even if the owner is not using his water, his fishing rights remain. Islanders worry that in selling land to "summer people," the islanders and their kinsmen will lose fishing rights, which they clearly regard as an insurance policy of sorts. Interestingly enough, if land is sold to an outsider, the new owner may not be allowed to go lobstering. Lobstering rights cannot be legally inherited or transferred in a deed.

CHAPTER 4

Territories

In midcoastal Maine, the area fished by one harbor gang is relatively small. In summer, when lobstermen are fishing "shedder bottom," they are rarely more than five miles from their harbors; in winter, when they fish deeper waters, they are seldom more than ten miles distant. A lobster fisherman thus spends his whole working life crossing and recrossing one small body of water. One herring fisherman says, "You show me a lobster fisherman fifty miles from home, and I'll show you a poor lost son of a bitch."

Each harbor where boats are moored ordinarily has its own harbor gang and lobster-fishing territory. (See map 2.) Usually there are as many territories associated with a township as there are harbors. A few of the largest harbors in the state have two gangs. In Friendship, for example, one gang has a territory to the west in Muscongus Bay, while another gang fishes the Georges Islands. Vinalhaven also has more than one territory. The waters around unoccupied islands near shore are normally included in nearby mainland fishing territories, but island waters farther out usually form special territories designated by the island name.

Fishermen talk about boundaries in terms of such key elements as river mouths, major peninsulas, and islands, but the actual dividing lines between lobstering territories are relatively small features fa-

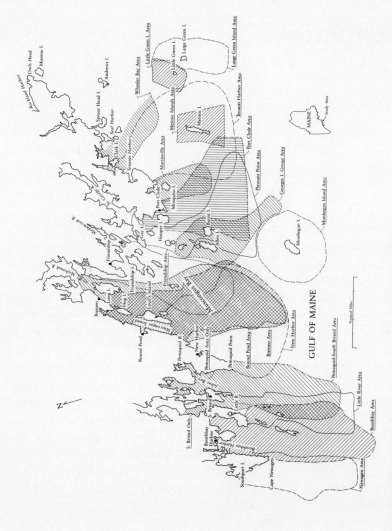

Map 2. Lobster fishing territories along the central Maine coast, 1982

miliar only to people intimately acquainted with the area. Along shore, boundaries are often marked by coves, small points, beaches, ledges, large trees on shore, or sea buoys. Offshore, fishermen make reference to islands or to underwater landmarks such as channels, ridges, or named locations. Offshore lines are now marked out with radar or loran much of the time.

Before the advent of such electronic gear, island territories were marked by reference to points on the mainland. The western boundary of Metinic Island is recognized when Whitehead, some six miles distant, is in line with the smokestack of the Thomaston Mill, twelve miles away.

Close to shore, boundaries are precise, defined to the yard. Offshore, they are less definite. In midwinter, miles from shore, there is a good deal of "mixed fishing" by individuals from different harbor gangs. In summer, when fishermen concentrate their traps near shore, they take care to place them on their own side of the boundary. At this time of year, when the productive area is far smaller, the influx of part-timers results in intense competition and fishermen monitor their boundaries closely.

Fishermen know about only those boundaries that affect them directly. Lobster fishermen from Bremen, for example, know the lines between their own territory and those of Friendship, Round Pond, and New Harbor, but they have only a vague idea of the boundaries between Pemaquid and South Bristol, harbors on the same peninsula. New Harbor fishermen are not even aware of the existence of the Georges Island area twelves miles from their home harbor. Lobstermen are also generally reluctant to talk about territoriality; it does, after all, involve trap cutting, which is an illegal activity.

Defense of Boundaries

Violation of territorial boundaries meets with no fixed response. An older person from an established family with a long history of fishing might infringe on the territorial rights of others almost indefinitely. Those being infringed upon are especially reluctant to accuse a gang leader or the member of a large family, either of whom could

have a large number of allies. An unpopular person, a young fisherman, or a newcomer encounters trouble more quickly. Sooner or
later, however, someone decides to take action against the inter-
loper. Sometimes a small group of fishermen decide to act in con-
cert, but boundary defense is often effected by one person acting
alone.

The violator is usually warned, sometimes by verbal threats and
abuse, but usually by surreptitious molestation of lobstering gear.
Two half-hitches of rope may be tied around the spindle of the buoy,
or legal-sized lobsters may be taken out and the doors of the traps
left open. Fishermen have been known to leave threatening notes in
bottles inside the offending traps, and one colorful islander carves a
representation of female genitalia in the styrofoam buoys. Most interlopers move their gear when warned in these ways. If the violations persist, the traps are destroyed. Fishermen have destroyed traps
by "carving them up a little" with a chain saw or by smashing them
with sledge hammers. When such traps are pulled, the owner has
little doubt as to what has happened. Usually, however, the offending traps are cut off: they are pulled, the buoy toggles and warp line
are cut, and the trap is pushed into deep water, where there is little
chance of finding it. There is no practical way to protect traps in the
water. Removing the traps not only removes the symbol of another
person's intrusion but also limits the intruder's capacity to reduce
the defender's own catch. Destruction of traps does not usually lead
to direct confrontation since the owner can only guess who destroyed them or even whether they were destroyed on purpose.

In a few instances, gangs defend their boundaries as a group. It is
well known that anyone invading the traditional territories of such
islands as Metinic, Monhegan, and Green Island can expect coordinated resistance from men fishing those islands. Once in a while,
groups goaded beyond endurance launch a full scale "cut war" in
which hundreds of traps are destroyed, boats sunk, and even docks
and fish houses burnt. These so-called lobster wars lead to long-
standing bitterness, violence, and court action.

It is a rare day in a harbor when someone does not suspect that his
traps have been tampered with. Many incidents occur as a result of
feuds and competition within a particular area. Much of this small-

scale molestation stems from the fact that maintaining territorial lines means constantly utilizing one's own territory and perhaps a little more—a process known as "pushing the lines." Even in slow months, a few traps are left in certain peripheral areas to maintain local territorial claims. However, fishermen touch another's gear only with great reluctance, knowing that their own gear is vulnerable to retaliation. The whole industry is aware that the individuals whose traps have been cut off may well take vengeance, but frequently against the wrong person. The result, they know, can be a comic and costly chain of events in which the innocent and the guilty retaliate blindly against one another. The norms are therefore widely obeyed, and although the entire coast is patrolled by only a few wardens, there is little trouble. Fishermen are very careful to punish intruders in ways that will not provoke a massive, violent response. According to one fisherman, "The trick to driving a man [out of the area] is to cut off just one or two traps at a time." This harassment makes it unprofitable to fish an area but does not challenge a man to open warfare, since he can only guess who cut his traps.

A conspiracy of silence surrounds all trap-cutting incidents and efforts to enforce boundaries. Those who resort to cutting traps rarely advertise their "skill with the knife," to reduce both the possibility of retaliation and the chance of losing their lobster licenses for destroying the traps of other men. Destruction of another's gear is always considered immoral, regardless of the circumstances, because it interferes with the victim's ability to feed his family. Victims may growl and threaten but they rarely report the incident to any law enforcement agency. The culprit's identity may be unknown, and chances of successful prosecution are small. Fishermen feel strongly that the law should be kept at bay and that people should handle their own problems. Any fisherman who goes to the police to complain about trap cuttings not only looks ineffectual and ridiculous but is somewhat of a threat. When a man's traps are missing, taking the law into his own hands is not only more effective but also maintains his standing among fellow fishermen.

Visitors to the Maine coast sometimes think that lobster fishermen are a bunch of surly outlaws. This impression is reinforced by tales of lobster wars in which hundreds of traps are cut off and property is destroyed. Widely repeated, these stories give the entire coast an unsavory reputation, which contains a kernel of truth. The territorial system does preempt a part of the public domain by groups that defend their claims by violence. But the stereotype concerning criminal behavior is essentially inaccurate. Fishermen obey the conservation laws. All register their boats and their trap buoy colors with the state of Maine; all have licenses. The prohibition against taking berried lobsters (with eggs) or "notch-tails" is universally obeyed.

The territorial system is a standard part of the social organization of the lobster-fishing industry. It is what Bailey (1969) calls an "encapsulated political system," operating with its own set of rules within a larger system. The boundaries are maintained by violence or threat, but the violence is patterned according to a codified set of rules.

Fishermen say that a man is allowed to fish within the entire territory owned by the harbor gang to which he belongs. This statement is not strictly accurate. A man is expected to keep his distance from other fishermen and not "dump" his traps on top of another's, where they can become entangled. Fishermen with traps in a saturated location have usufructuary rights; others cannot enter until someone leaves. The older, more skilled fishermen are likely to have their traps prepositioned in the best locations. When lobsters do appear, those who have "camped out" in good spots have monopolized all or most of the available space. Younger fishermen—particularly those who have joined the gang recently—are well advised to stay out of the way of men with status in the hierarchy of skill and prestige. Men of lower status can lose a great deal by coming into conflict with highliners.

Sometimes groups of men use a particular spot or set of spots for such a long time that they begin to feel proprietary rights over these locations. Within harbor gangs in the study area, however, such men have only usufructuary rights, not permanent ownership. Should the men who regularly fish in a location move their traps elsewhere, others from the harbor gang can move their traps into it. Under unusual circumstances men attempt to maintain small private domains within a gang's territory. A boat builder on one of the offshore islands maintained a private area off his own property where he alone placed traps. If anyone else placed traps in his preserve, he would cut off their traps, pull up all his own fishing gear, and go to work building boats until trouble died down. To the best of my knowledge, no individual areas of this kind existed in any harbor gang in the midcoastal region in the 1980s.

It is much more common for part-time fishermen and those low on the prestige scale to be restricted to certain areas. Two part-time fishermen have said that they place traps only in the coves where they own cottages. They have had no difficulty, in part because of the idea that ownership of land gives fishing rights in adjacent waters. They can also keep an eye on some of their gear. Both, however, have received definite hints that they would experience trouble if they tried to fish elsewhere in the gang's territory.

Boundary Movement

During the past sixty years, all boundaries have moved somewhat, but at varying rates of speed. Some have been surprisingly stable. The boundary line between Tenants Harbor and Martinsville has moved less than a mile since 1920. In other areas, especially in the western part of this zone, boundary movement has been much faster.

Boundary movement often occurs as a result of incremental, nonviolent encroachment by individuals on the area of another gang. During the spring of 1971, for example, one ledge in the New Harbor territory was being fished by two men from that town. In early July, three fishermen from Friendship, where the number of fishermen was increasing, also began to fish there. After several weeks, the New Harbor fishermen moved their traps from the area, angrily declaring that the spot was so "polluted with traps" that it was not worthwhile to fish there any longer. Other Friendship fishermen moved in. By the end of that year, mixed fishing was allowed.

In a few instances, boundary movement is the result of coordinated, violent action by a group of men. One such incident occurred in the mid 1950s, when a group of Tenants Harbor fishermen decided to fish an area off the privately owned Penobscot Bay islands. Their traps were promptly cut off; they retaliated in kind, and for a few weeks a minor "war" broke loose. Over the course of a summer, Tenants Harbor fishermen succeeded in making life so miserable for the islanders that they were able to push the line back a few hundred yards. Violence, however, does not always lead to boundary movement. Over several decades, various groups have transgressed the Green Island boundary, which nevertheless has continued in place.

Rapid boundary movement can take place without violence, as when islanders move to the mainland or sell the island to a tourist who either does not know the value of the traditional lobster-fishing area or cannot defend it. The area is then quickly incorporated into the fishing territories of adjacent harbors. In the past few years, Teal Island in Muscongus Bay was sold to outsiders, and its fishing area was taken over by Pleasant Point and Port Clyde; the Loud's Island area was incorporated by Bremen and Round Pond.

Not all islands abandoned by their fishermen are peacefully incorporated into the territory of another harbor gang. Isle au Haut affords a case in point. In the 1950s fishermen lived on the island and maintained their own area, but in the following decade, these men moved to nearby towns on the mainland. They continued to fish around the island and defended their area successfully until the mid 1980s. Trouble has erupted as Stonington fishermen encroach on the area. One boat reportedly has been sunk, and a number of traps have been cut off. In time this subzone will probably be incorporated into the Stonington area.

Boundary movements are rarely the result of individual actions. If only two individuals are involved in a dispute, a stalemate is likely to result. Fishermen have said that "two men who get to fighting only put each other out of business." Such statements, however, are not completely accurate. If a person is determined to remain in an area, he can make it very expensive for anyone who wants to dislodge him. In one night, a single person can destroy more traps than several people can set. Reportedly large-scale trap cutting has been accomplished by attaching a scythe to the side of a boat and running the boat close to the offending warp lines. In local legend, hundreds of traps have been thus destroyed by one person in the course of a night.

The decision to defend or to intrude on the area of another gang depends on a hard-headed assessment of benefits and costs. A large bay up one of the tidewater rivers is the exclusive fishing ground of one man and his family, who defend the area against all comers. Their defense of the area is strengthened by the famiiy's reputation for violence and by the fact that some members have spent an unusual amount of time in jail. (One of my research assistants, on a boat that supposedly invaded this family area, witnessed a hammer being thrown through the boat's windshield.) Members of this famiily say that the lobster population in the area can support only a few fishermen, and since their small boats cannot operate outside the river, other fishermen should leave their paltry supply alone. But the maintenance and observance of boundaries are always based on rationality. Where honor and feelings of self-worth are at stake, men have not always acted in their best economic interests. Most forays, however, especially those involving the kind of long-term actions necessary to change territorial boundaries, are made with a clear eye to economic benefit.

A Tyopology of Territories

There are two different types of lobster-fishing territories in mid-coastal Maine. Although fishermen are aware of the difference between them, they have no terminology to describe what I call "nucleated" and "perimeter-defended areas."[1] Nucleated areas are defined in terms of the major harbor where fishing vessels are moored, perimeter-defended areas in terms of the peripheral boundaries. Nucleated areas exist in the mainland harbors in the western part of the study area, from the Sheepscot River to Port Clyde. Perimeter-defended areas exist only in the fishing waters surrounding Green Island, Matinicus, Metinic, Monhegan and some of the smaller islands in the Muscle Ridge channel.

In nucleated areas the fishermen's sense of territoriality is proportional to the distance from the harbor. Intruding traps placed near the harbor mouth are quickly destroyed. On the periphery, the sense of territoriality is weak and a good deal of mixed fishing takes place. In Muscongus Bay, for example, the fishermen from New Harbor,

Round Pond, Bremen, and Friendship have exclusive fishing zones near their own home harbors, but in the cold months of the year, when they fish in the middle of the bay, men from these harbors fish together. Yet the areas on the boundaries of nucleated areas cannot be exploited by fishermen from just any harbor. Mixed fishing does not imply completely open access. Were fishermen from Monhegan, Tenants Harbor, or Boothbay to place traps in the middle of Muscongus Bay, they would almost certainly have trouble.

With perimeter-defended areas, the sense of ownership remains strong out to the boundaries of the territory. Boundaries are sharply defined and defended to the yard. There is little mixed fishing. Fishermen feel that if they are going to keep people from other harbor gangs on one side of the boundary, they should stay on their own side. Even in the winter months fishermen rarely fish outside the area they claim for their exclusive use.

As noted earlier, it is easier to gain acceptance in mainland harbor gangs, where nucleated fishing areas are found, than on the islands, with their perimeter-defended territories. The barriers to entering harbor gangs that fish perimeter-defended areas are to be expected, given the nature of their defensive boundary arrangements. The object of maintaining impermeable boundaries is to reduce the number of people fishing in an area. There is no sense in incurring the cost of defending strict boundaries if anyone can join the harbor gang. Thus, fishermen who strongly defend their boundaries against other harbor gangs also limit entry into their own gangs to a much greater extent than do those fishing nucleated areas. As a consequence there are fewer fishermen per square mile of fishing area in perimeter defended areas, which produces both biological and economic benefits. Most important, lobsters taken from perimeter-defended areas are consistently larger, and catches and catches per unit of effort are greater. In addition, fishermen from these areas earn significantly higher incomes (see Appendix).

In the early decades of the century, according to older informants, all lobstering areas in the midcoastal region were essentially perimeter-defended. The nucleated areas, now predominant, are a relatively recent phenomenon, which have come about as the boundaries between small areas have been pushed back or have broken down completely, with the resultant amalgamation of several small areas into larger, nucleated fishing territories. Before 1920, lobstering was done only in summer in very small territories held by groups of men who defended them vigorously. This fishing pattern was connected in part to the technology of the day. Fishing was done from a small sloop or rowing dory, which could not be used safely in stormy weather. The area that a man could fish was very restricted, as was the effective travel radius, and the amount of "lobster bottom" that a fisherman could learn with a lead line was very limited. Since the income of these harbor gangs depended on a very small area, territory was jealously guarded. Many of these small fishing areas were also adjacent to legally owned land holdings, and at that time the idea that landowners had a right to the "shedder bottom" or "short-warp fishing" off their property was unquestioned.[2]

These perimeter-defended areas have lasted to the present around the islands in Penobscot Bay. In the western part of the central Maine coast, the small perimeter-defended areas have been combined into larger nucleated areas, mostly fished by people from at least two harbors.

The breakdown of the small, perimeter-defended territories was made possible by technological change. As motors came into common use in the 1930s, small skiffs and dories give way to larger, faster boats. The introduction of depth-sounding equipment in 1950 made it easier to learn the bottom. Both innovations greatly increased the area a fisherman could exploit effectively.

Reasons for the differential breakdown of boundaries around the perimeter-defended areas must also be sought in ecological and political factors. In the western part of the study area, where the coast is convoluted into deep bays and long peninsulas, harbor gangs from communities on the ends of peninsulas have been under considerable pressure from those further up the rivers and bays. In the days of sail, fishermen from communities up the estuaries restricted their fishing to summer and exploited the waters directly adjacent to their home harbors. As late as the early 1960s, most of the men from such towns were content to be part-time fishermen with small boats. Since the 1970s, these men have had to fish full-time in order to survive economically. To gain access to deep water and winter lobster concentrations, they have been buying bigger boats to reach areas formerly exclusive to the peninsular towns. Such individuals sacrifice a great deal to gain access to open-ocean fishing areas. Their alternative is to be restricted to shallow waters around their home harbors and to fish only during the summer.

For people in harbors on the open sea, it has not been worthwhile to repel the invaders. While incursions from upriver communities mean more competition and a subsequent reduction in both catches and revenues, attempts to stop the invasions would cause a great deal of trouble, perhaps even a full-fledged lobster war, with huge financial losses, problems with the law, and worse. Thus, harbor gangs from places such as New Harbor, Boothbay Harbor, and South Bristol now operate in nucleated areas, with small zones near the mouth of their harbors for their exclusive use, and share a great deal of the deep waters in the bays with fishermen from inland towns. The amount of mixed fishing is especially large in fall, winter, and spring, when individuals from river and bay towns must come "outside" to fish at all.

Perimeter-defended areas around Penobscot Bay islands have survived because their defenders have so far been able to cope with incursions. Two factors have bolstered the islanders' defense. First, the men from mainland harbors have not been particularly aggressive in pushing into the areas controlled by island harbor gangs. Harbor gangs from towns such as Tenants Harbor, Port Clyde, and Spruce Head have access both to shoals and to deep water; their fishermen can operate year-round without going far from home or encroaching on neighboring island gangs. Second, men fishing the island areas have been willing to mount a spirited defense of their areas, despite the smaller number of gang members. It is common knowledge that anyone who attempts to fish in the area around Monhegan, Green Island, or Criehaven will meet with coordinated resistance from the island men. Especially in islands owned by families, long-term ownership lends strong moral overtones to their claims. Gangs fishing permanently occupied islands have mustered effective defenses in part because the mutual interdependence of island living fosters a sense of identity and exclusiveness, bringing individual behavior under more control. Moreover, a loss of fishing grounds is a direct threat to the livelihood of most island families. The ability of leaders such as the king to coordinate defensive activities is also enhanced by these factors.

Distance does not play a key role in maintaining these perimeter-defended areas. The men who fish off some of these islands (e.g., Green Island, Little Green island, and Metinic) actually live on the mainland and make the trip daily to these islands to fish. In addition, lobster fishermen from mainland harbors commonly go more than twenty miles in search of lobsters and sometimes go as far as Cashes Ledge, fifty miles away, for a few hauls in the spring.

The size of the harbor gang is not a factor in the defense of an area. Virtually all the mainland harbors have more fishermen than the island harbor gangs. The islanders, however, can mobilize more men "on the line," so to speak, than the larger mainland harbor gangs. This ability is what counts.

The present disposition of lobster-fishing territories is a function of the costs and benefits of territorial defense. On the mainland, men in harbors on the ends of peninsulas have not found it worthwhile to defend their territorial boundaries against more desperate men from upriver. As a result boundaries have broken down and the area where mixed fishing is allowed has increased. These processes have produced nucleated areas on the mainland. On the island areas in Penobscot Bay, fishermen have maintained boundaries, and perimeter-defended territory continues to be the rule.

CHAPTER 5

Tricks of the Trade

Lobstering is carried out in boats ranging from small, unpowered skiffs to 45-foot vessels. Most skiffs range from 14 to 20 feet in length and are powered by two-cycle outboard motors of 18 to 25 horsepower. Skiff fishermen operate primarily during the summer. Full-time commercial fishermen are likely to have boats 33 to 36 feet in length, powered by gas or diesel engines, although both smaller and larger vessels are found in large numbers.

There are some very real limits on lobster-boat size. No full-time fishermen operate boats under 26 feet, because boats of this size are too small to transport sufficient numbers of traps efficiently and can be operated only in calm seas. Boats over 42 feet long are rarely found in the inshore lobster fishery, as they are too large to be efficient. A man can pull the same number of traps in a day with a 32-foot boat for far less cost in terms of fuel, depreciation, and maintenance. Virtually the only boats in the lobster fishery over 42 feet are those used for lobstering on the offshore areas such as Cashes Ledge or Georges Bank or those used to fish for another species during part of the year.

Traditional lobster boats were constructed of wood. Fiberglass boats have become common since 1970, because of performance characteristics and easier maintenance. Most lobster boats are built in Maine boatyards, although a few boats from Nova Scotia ("Novie boats") are in use. Allowing for minor design variations, the Maine lobster boat has a high bow, making it relatively seaworthy when headed into the wind. Back of the cabin, the stern and sides are low so that lobster pots can easily be hauled aboard, and to minimize wind action when the boat is broadside. Because the keel does not extend all the way to the stern of the boat, the turning radius is smaller, which increases maneuverability for picking up lobster buoys. (See figure 3.)

A lobster boat is usually equipped with a hydraulic hauler for pulling lobster traps to the surface, a depth finder, a citizen's band radio, and containers for bait and captured lobsters. An increasing number of boats have radar, VHF, and loran C, but these are not standard equipment. Each of these devices helps fisherman in different ways. Radios and radar increase safety. The depth finders help a fisherman to learn the bottom and aid in placing traps. Loran C, which is a very precise navigational instrument, helps a fisherman find particular fishing locations, place strings of traps, and find his way to and from the fishing grounds. Many lobster boats have a small mast near the stern to allow the use of a sail on windy days. The sail helps keep the boat headed into the wind and reduces the effects of wave motion, thus providing a more stable work platform.

Since most lobster boats are intended as inshore day-fishing vessels, they rarely have bunks, stoves, toilets, or even freshwater tanks. They are usually designed to be operated by a single man, although sternmen are commonly employed during the busy fall months.

Lobster traps or pots are relatively uniform along the entire coast. They are made of either wood or metal wire. The traditional wooden lobster traps have flat bottoms but may be rounded or rectangular. They are usually three or four feet long and constructed of oak frames covered with spruce laths, which are placed about an inch and three quarters apart to allow water circulation and still retain legal-size lobsters. Metal wire traps are being used with greater frequency. Constructed of vinyl-coated or galvanized aluminum wire and rectangular in shape, they are ordinarily four feet long. The open end (or ends) contains a funnel-shaped nylon net or "head" that allows lobsters to enter the trap. An extra head across the center of

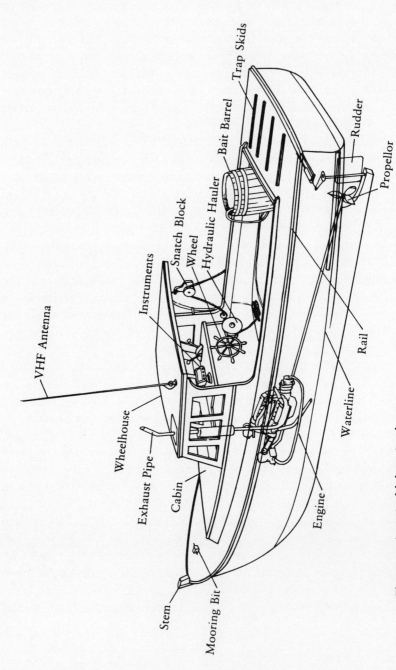

Figure 3. A typical lobstering boat

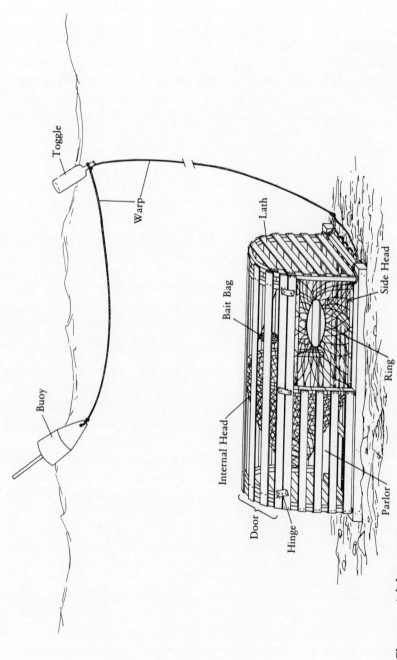

Figure 4. A lobster trap

the trap, called a parlor head, is meant to decrease the possibility of escape. (See figure 4.)

Bait ordinarily consists of fish frames or herring remnants obtained from nearby fish-processing plants. Sometimes whole fresh fish such as menhaden and herring are used. The bait is placed inside the trap, usually just behind the entry heads. The herring remnants are put in small string bags (bagged bait) and tied in position. Fish frames are first stuck on a baiting iron, which has a hole in the tip. To bait the trap, the end of the bait string, which is attached to the bottom of the trap, is placed through the hole of the bait iron. The bait is then pushed on to the bait string, and the trap is closed and ready to be placed.

Lobster traps are attached to Styrofoam buoys by a nylon or hemp rope called a warp, which is measured in fathoms (six feet). The length of the warp varies from ten to sixty fathoms, depending on the depth of water and time of year. Each trap a person puts out must have his identification number. In most areas, one or two traps are attached to a single buoy—practices termed fishing singles or fishing doubles—but between Pemaquid Point and Cape Elizabeth to the west, is it legal and customary to "fish trawls," by attaching six to ten traps to one warp. By putting buoys only on the ends of the trawl lines and laying the gear roughly in a north-south direction, fishermen attempt to reduce the possibility of entangling their gear with another's. Fishermen normally place traps in the water in strings or long rows so that they can see from one buoy to another in the fog.

The number of traps a man can pull depends greatly on the weather, since wave action makes it difficult to spot buoys and handle traps. When the weather is good, a fisherman fishing singles or doubles might pull about two hundred traps; a man and a sternman fishing trawls might pull three hundred fifty or more. In the summer, traps may be pulled every day; in the winter when the weather is bad and lobsters are more difficult to catch, traps may be pulled only once a week or even less frequently.

The number of traps that lobstermen use in the midcoastal region varies tremendously. Some part-time skiff fishermen might have as few as ten traps. Full-time fishermen in the area typically use three to five hundred. In the study area, the number of traps tends to be smaller east of Pemaquid Point, where trawl fishing is outlawed.

Larger numbers tend to be used in South Bristol and the Boothbay region, where fishing trawls is standard. Further west, in the Portland and Casco Bay region (outside the study area), even larger gangs of traps are the rule. In this area fishermen, aided by one or two sternmen, may fish up to twenty-five hundred traps.

Investment in lobster fishing has increased substantially in the past few years because of inflation, the use of larger boats and more sophisticated electronic gear, and the escalating numbers of traps. In some harbors, the shift to the more expensive metal traps has also increased fishermen's costs. In 1987, a fully equipped inboard powered boat cost $35,000 at a minimum. Traps cost $25 each; the line or warp cost extra. A pickup truck, dock, workshop, and tools exceeded $40,000. There is an enormous variation in investment. Beginning lobster fishermen usually had a small number of traps, used boats, and equipment costing under $10,000 in the early 1980s. Well-established fishermen with large, well-equipped boats, large docks, large numbers of traps, a truck, and a workshop could have $200,000 invested in their business.

Fishermen must purchase a state license before they can go lobster fishing; up to 1987 such licenses were being given to all comers for a nominal fee. All traps must have the owner's license number on them. Each fishermen's trap buoys must be painted a distinctive set of colors registered with the Maine Department of Marine Resources. Color coding makes it easy for fishermen to distinguish their traps from others and helps enforce the law that prohibits pulling another's traps. Fishermen usually choose bright yellows, pinks, and whites, or dark and light stripes to make it easier to identify buoys from a distance, and in the fog.

Several important laws passed by the Maine legislature protect the breeding stock. Legal-size lobsters must be between $3\frac{3}{16}$ and 5 inches on the carapace: smaller lobsters are sexually immature, while larger ones are breeding stock. It is illegal to take a berried female with eggs on her abdomen. When a fisherman catches a berried female, he may voluntarily cut a notch in the right tail flipper and return her to the water. Once they are notch-tailed, females cannot be legally taken, for they are proven breeding stock.

All lobster traps in Maine must be equipped with a vent of $1\frac{3}{4}$ inches to allow undersized lobsters to escape and reduce their mortality from handling and cannibalism. In 1986, a new law went into effect requiring that an escape hatch, made of biodegradable material, be built into every trap. This prevents lobsters from being trapped in "ghost" traps—lost traps which it is thought continue to fish.

These regulations are strongly supported by the lobster industry and almost universally obeyed. People do not go fishing without a license, and the laws pertaining to legal sizes and berried females are not intentionally violated by most fishermen. In addition, many fishermen cut notches in the flippers of berried females to insure that they will not be taken by other fishermen in the future. Fishermen feel that the new vent law is a good one and comply with it. The only fishing regulation that appears to be violated with regularity is the law protecting oversize lobsters. I have never seen fishermen take oversize females, because it is recognized that they are essential to maintain the breeding stock. Oversized males are another matter. I have seen a number of them taken home "to feed the family."

Lobster management is currently in a state of flux. The controversial Lobster Management Plan of the New England Regional Fisheries Management Council calls for standardizing lobster regulations all along the East Coast. This plan would increase the minimum size from 3³⁄₁₆ to 3½, ostensibly allowing a much higher percentage of lobsters to molt into sizes where they could breed at least once before capture. It would also abolish the laws against taking notched lobsters and lobsters over five inches on the carapace. There is currently a good deal of controversy and political maneuvering over these proposed changes. A bill embodying all these changes is scheduled to become law on January 1, 1988. Given the amount of political maneuvering taking place in 1987, it could conceivably be scuttled.

Skills

Lobstermen everywhere spend countless hours together talking about weather, seasons, fishing gear, and related matters, and many more hours alone wondering about fishing locations, the competition, and what changes they might make to improve catches.

When the novice starts to discuss the behavior of lobsters and the factors influencing catches, he finds himself in a strange and technical subculture. At first, the outsider can pick up no discernible pattern in the conversations and technical talk. Dialogue among lobster fishermen resembles nothing so much as subterranean tours in and around ridges, holes, ledges, and seaweed-covered slopes. Generalizations are rare. Discussions about fishing quickly settle into tales of curious experiences on various "bottoms," the minutiae of lobster behavior, or detailed catalogues of equipment.

How important are fishing knowledge and skills? Fishermen disagree, sometimes sharply. They concede generally that their incomes are affected by a combination of factors including capital and effort, but in the minds of many, knowledge and skill play an important role. "Some men," they say, "know how to catch lobsters. Others don't." In every harbor, fishermen tell stories of individuals who can outfish anyone else, even with an old boat and a small gang of traps.

Dealers and fish buyers confirm that some men earn more than others using the same equipment in the same area. They note that several novice fishermen with good boats and equipment have gone out of business because they did not know how to use these resources to full advantage.

Though the evidence is subject to qualification, one of our earliest studies demonstrates that the income of lobster fishermen cannot be explained solely in terms of capital equipment and effort.[1] In fact, many fishermen consider skills and knowledge so important that a conspiracy of silence surrounds these matters. Some men simply do not talk about factors influencing catches. As one lobsterman put it, "You are asking the secret of how I earn my living." Successful fishermen try hard to obscure exactly what they are doing.

Beyond the basic skills involved in piloting and maintenance, experienced fishermen focus on issues directly affecting lobster catches, particularly skills in trap placement. One old man is fond of saying, "The old-timers know how to make their traps count; the kids are just throwing them all over the bay." Fishermen generally

agree that building a proper trap and using bait correctly are also vital skills, but are not as important as placement.[2]

Because the working environment is so uncertain, all fishermen
have some degree of ignorance. Much of the knowledge in lobster
fishing involves information about the behavior of the lobster itself—a subject far more difficult to study than animals in a pasture,
which can be observed at close range.

According to fishermen, lobsters are not evenly spread over the
entire bottom. They are concentrated in specific areas, and those
concentrations change according to the season. Although every lobsterman has a lot of ideas about the behavior of the creatures, there is
surprising unanimity among experienced fishermen, and the weight
of biological evidence supports their composite view.

Fishermen state that a large proportion of all lobsters molting into
legal size are caught within the span of a few months. The best fishing is in the late summer and early fall, just after the lobsters have
shed. The lobsters then are not only numerous but eat voraciously
to "fill out their shells." One lobster fisherman said he would like it
to "be October all year." In early winter, catches fall off, because of
the effects of fishing and because lobsters are inactive in the colder
water. The creatures become more active in the spring and more of
them crawl into traps, but because a large proportion of legal-size
lobsters have already been captured, catches are not as good as in
the fall.

Fishermen move their traps in accordance with the patterns of
lobster movement and the type of ocean bottom. Fisherman describe
the bottom as a series of ridges or shoals separated by valleys or
channels. In some places, shoals are quite broad. On the shoals is
hard bottom, generally composed of rocks covered with kelp. Deeper,
"down off the hard bottom," are gravel, then sand, and finally, at the
bottom, mud.

Depending on the season, say fishermen, lobsters are found at different depths and on different types of bottom. In the summer, lobsters move to very shallow water to shed; there they burrow in the
mud or hide in rocky areas along shore. After shedding, they head for
deeper water, traveling over sand and gravel because this type of bottom affords the fewest obstacles. As they move into deeper water,

lobsters like to hug the edge of the shoals, going relatively fast on the sand and gravel and staying close to rocky hiding places. During the fall and spring migrations, therefore, many fishermen place large numbers of traps on "the edge," where hard and soft bottom meet.

During late fall and winter hibernation, lobsters again burrow in the mud or in hiding places on rocky bottom and tend to stay in one place. Skilled lobstermen state that lobsters prefer places where the bottom is irregular. Mounds and rock piles yield more lobsters than flat rocky areas, and muddy bottoms with occasional rocks and breaks in the contours are more productive than flat mud or sandy surfaces. Lobsters may concentrate in certain areas for no discernible reason, one year on one type of bottom at a particular location, another year on the same type of bottom but in a different place. According to several good lobstermen, lobsters avoid shallow areas with "white, bald rocks" because there is no kelp to hide in.

Fishermen believe that the "working time" of the bait has an enormous effect on catches, varying considerably with the time of year. In the summer, traps need to be pulled every two or three days, since lobsters are very active. The bait then lasts only a few days at the most because "everything is eating it." In the winter, fishermen tend their traps less frequently, and the bait lasts longer. Most fishermen do not use spoiled bait. The test is to throw it overboard: if it floats, it is "bad." (To the amateur, it all smells bad of course.)

Biologists familiar with the lobster agree that catches vary markedly over the course of the year, for precisely the same reasons as suggested by fishermen. Krouse (1973: 172), among others, points out that over 90 percent of the lobsters molting into legal size are caught within a year. The number of legal-size lobsters is largest in the weeks after shedding, and the availability of lobsters decreases as the year goes on. By late spring, few legal-size lobsters are left in coastal waters. Biologists are also certain that lobsters are easier to trap in late summer, fall, and spring than in winter because their activity level varies with water temperature (Paloheimo 1963: 62), and that catches are likely to be very low in June and early July, when the creatures are hiding in the rocks and shedding. Our data reinforce these assertions (Acheson 1980c: 653).

The weight of biological evidence supports the fishermen's contention that lobsters prefer rock areas, even though they may burrow in the mud and sand, and that they prefer less bottom material (Cobb 1971: 112–114). Biological evidence, though inconsistent concerning the assertion that lobsters migrate seasonally, does seem to support this conclusion. Tagging experiments carried out by Cooper and Uzmann (1971: 288) demonstrate shoalward migration in the spring and summer and a return to the edge of the shelf in the fall and winter.

Our own data generally support the fishermen's conviction that traps must be moved seasonally (Acheson 1980b: table 12) and that hard bottom is the most productive over the course of the year. Our data also supported their belief that lobster concentrations, vary greatly even in relatively small areas (Acheson 1980c: 663–66). There is no consensus on the reason for the phenomenon, among either fishermen or biologists. According to Tom Morrissey (personal communication 1979) of the National Marine Fisheries Service, "All of a sudden, one area will do very well for a few years, and then return to normal. Probably a maze of environmental factors is involved."

Scientific studies have also shown that lobster populations are low in areas with little kelp (Mann and Breen 1972). Four other biologists I interviewed (Jim Thomas of the Maine Department of Marine Resources, Dave Dean, Hugh Dewitt, and Bob Bayer of the University of Maine) agree that traps come to peak productivity more quickly in summer than in fall or spring. Again, their explanations are the same as those offered by fishermen, although they came to their conclusions by a different process.

Experienced fishermen are far less unanimous about trap construction than about trap placement. Between 1977 and 1979, when our data were collected, fishermen were arguing about the effect on catches of trap construction material, length of traps, and types of heads. Some men asserted that traps made from aluminized or vinyl-covered wire, which had recently been introduced, fished better than wooden traps. Our data indicated that the trap construction material unquestionably had some effect on catch levels. On the whole, aluminized wire traps performed better than vinyl-coated wire traps and than wooden traps (Acheson 1980b: Table 11). Some men, however, did better with wooden traps, and in the spring there were no statistically significant differences among traps made from the three materials. Fishermen explain the superiority of metal traps in terms of stability. Wooden traps, even those with weights, tend to float and move because of wave and tidal action. Lobsters, they claim, prefer to crawl into the more stationary metal traps. A few fishermen think that lobsters may be attracted by the bright metal wire of the aluminized traps rather than the duller wooden and vinyl-wire traps. Others assert that lobsters are probably repelled by the smell of the vinyl-covered wire.

All biologists interviewed believed that trap-construction material could have an appreciable effect on catches but none had any experience with the issue. On the whole, the biologists' explanations for the success of metal traps overlapped considerably with those of fishermen.

Some lobster fishermen believed that four-foot traps outfished three-foot traps; other equally skilled men stated that trap length made no appreciable difference. Our catch data indicated that in every season four-foot traps did substantially better than three-foot ones. The difference was greatest in the summer, when four-foot traps produced 0.6242 pounds/trap/layover day, while the three-foot traps caught an average of only 0.3079 pounds/trap/layover day (Acheson 1980c: table 10). Men fishing three-foot traps were disturbed, dubious, and incredulous when shown these figures. The four-foot advocates were gratified, although several did ask us not to spread the word to other fishermen. Fishermen convinced of the virtues of four-foot traps offer two reasons. First, such traps have an extra head and thus make it more difficult for the lobster to escape. Second, because traps are larger, the defensive behavior of a lobster caught in one of them is less likely to prevent another from entering. The biologists agreed with the first argument but not the second.

Fishermen also argued the virtues of different trap heads. In the late 1970s, the argument was between the advocates of hog-ring heads and hake-mouth heads. Hake-mouth heads are made entirely of string pulled tight to restrict the size of the opening; hog-ring heads have a metal hoop, about six inches in diameter, attached to the mouths of the heads. Advocates of hog-ring heads believe that it makes a trap easy for the lobster to enter and that once inside, lobsters have a hard time finding their way out. The secret of a good trap is to make entry easy. The "hake-mouth" advocates say lobsters can crawl into traps with ease and are bright enough to escape through anything but the narrowest opening, such as a hake-mouth head.

Respect for the intelligence of the lobster has grown. In the last few decades, many fishermen have shifted from hog-ring to hake-mouth heads, or to traps with hog rings in the side heads and hake mouths on the interior. Most skilled fishermen believe these traps with mixed heads are superior, though other fishermen use only hake-mouth heads throughout. The data my crew collected support the idea that traps with mixed heads are the best, followed by those with hake mouths. Hog-ring traps were least successful (Acheson 1980b: 23–24). Because these results were not statistically significant, however, fishermen may have a real cause for disagreement. The same biologists saw very little unusual in these results. Two biologists clearly agreed with the fishermen's explanation for the superiority of mixed heads.

The availability of bait differs seasonally, and dealers and cooperatives do not always stock all varieties. Redfish can usually be obtained at all times of year. Herring and poggies (menhaden) can be obtained only in the summer and fall, while alewives are available only in the spring. Dogfish and so-called fresh dragged bait (i.e., cod, hake, haddock, and so on) are available periodically all year. Dragged bait is often well on its way to being spoiled.

There is a partial consensus among fishermen that the best bait is a combination of bagged herring and redfish, followed by redfish alone, herring, or poggies. The poorest bait is dragged bait and dogfish. Some fishermen do a little gill netting in the summer to cut costs and increase variety. On a given day, they usually have only one type of bait on board.

Again our catch data bear out the fishermen's predictions about the productivity of the different baits (Acheson 1980c: 676–78). In the fall and spring, combined herring and redfish do best, while dragged bait is least productive. The only contradictory result was that during the summer, dragged bait (which many fishermen believe to be highly undesirable) did better than herring. Frozen alewives, as many fishermen predicted, did the worst. Fishermen do not always use redfish or herring, however. Some switch bait periodically, claiming that not all lobsters like the same bait, while others never fish the kinds of bait used by the men nearest them, believing that lobsters grow bored with particular baits.

The biologists had far less to say about bait than the fishermen did, but their statements generally confirmed fishermen's views. All four biologists pointed out that there is no reason to suspect that all baits would be equally productive. One agreed that lobsters, like any other animals, have food preferences.

Two comments by biologists stand in general contradiction to fishermen's beliefs. Dave Dean mentioned studies demonstrating that lobsters like dragged bait. Jim Thomas (personal communication 1979) said that he believed that bait made no significant difference in total catches. When lobsters were hungry they would eat what was available, even if they did have their preferred foods. In eastern Maine, he said, bagged herring is used as a bait almost exclusively, while in the central part of the state all kinds of bait were used, including herring. There is no difference in catch per unit of effort between these areas.

Fishermen's statements about factors influencing catches and lobster behavior, though not scientific, do not seem preposterous to biologists familiar with the lobster industry. Quite the contrary, in most cases fishermen and biologists are in close agreement.

One difference did become apparent in our interviews. Fishermen have a good idea what influences the efficiency of their traps and catches in the short run (e.g., bait and trap position) but far less information about factors influencing long-run lobster population trends. Moreover, their opinions on such matters are both more speculative and more diffuse than those of biologists.

Analysis of data and interviews with both fishermen and biologists provide insight into the factors influencing catches, but a great deal remains to be explained—in particular the unexplained variance in analysis of the lobster-catch data.[3]

Trap Placement

Fishermen place their traps where they believe they will catch a maximum number of lobsters, at the same time minimizing the chance of losing traps. Fishermen never place their traps in water so shallow as to expose them at low tide. Lobsters are likely to die in exposed traps, and such traps can be vandalized. Also, lobstermen rarely place traps in water deeper than forty-five fathoms, because the cost of forty fathoms of warp is too high relative to the expected catch. Traps are not put in water that is too deep for the amount of warp line or where the tide current is so swift that the trap buoy is pulled under water. A trap placed "over its head" is usually lost for good. For similar reasons, fishermen take care not to place traps with relatively short warps where the current might drag them into deep holes. Unskilled fishermen sometimes try to minimize such trap losses by keeping extralong warps on all their traps. More skilled fishermen usually avoid this practice because very long warps easily become entangled with other traps. The exact warp length that experienced men leave depends on the depth, the current, and the number of traps nearby.

Weather is another factor in trap placement. In a storm, wave action can destroy traps that are placed in shallow water close to ledges. Fishermen therefore do not place traps in shallow water or near offshore ledges from late fall until the end of April, although they cannot completely avoid such spots without abandoning some of the best fishing areas. Fishermen working in shallow water minimize trap losses by avoiding areas where storms can cause the most turbulence, by keeping a weather eye open, and by putting in long hours moving traps when storms are imminent. The size of a person's boat also plays a role, since men whose boats have a large carrying capacity can rescue more traps when storms threaten.

Experienced fishermen are successful at "working around the ledges," but novices typically lost traps. Trap losses can also be reduced by taking care to avoid shipping lanes or "tows" frequented by draggers; traps can be lost by being dragged up in nets or having their warps cut by propellers.

To maximize the catch, fishermen need to put traps in microecological niches where lobsters are concentrated. Just after the lobsters shed, fishermen place most of their traps in shallow areas close to shore or on shallow ledges. When lobsters begin to migrate offshore in the late summer and early fall, fishermen place many of their traps on the gravel bottom or along the edge of hard bottom—

the "migration routes." In the winter, traps are generally placed in relatively deep water (fifteen to forty fathoms) in mud or rocky bottom.

Lobsters do not move at a steady pace over the bottom. Sometimes fishermen can keep a string of traps in the same location for two weeks or longer; at other times they must move them almost constantly to keep up with the migrating lobsters. The trick, as several highliners have said, is to keep just ahead of them. By keeping his strings ahead of the lobsters (and other fishermen), a man is better able to reserve the choice trap locations for himself. Moreover, if the traps cannot be pulled for a few days because of bad weather, they will still be productive.

Most fishermen phrase their placement strategy in terms of depth and bottom. They say, "We are going to place traps on hard bottom at ten fathoms," or "This string is going down the middle of the channel on the mud bottom at twenty to twenty-five fathoms," or "There is a little hole here and I am going to put these all around the edge of it." Skilled fishermen can pinpoint placement of their traps. One lobsterman I know keeps a trap in a large crevice within ten feet of shore; it produces a lobster a day from mid July to mid August.

Enormous piloting skill is necessary to maneuver around the offshore ledges, white with breaking surf, to manipulate a large bouncing boat next to a rocky crevice without sustaining serious damage. One day I went with Ed Drisko of New Harbor, who said he was going to place his traps at thirteen fathoms all day long. During the day we went over much of Muscongus Bay. At the end of the day, a look at his depth recorder showed that we had been in waters twelve to fifteen fathoms deep at least 90 percent of the time.

Experienced lobstermen use their depth-recording equipment to locate various types of bottom or specific features when the visibility is limited. A man placing traps circles in a hundred-yard area, intently looking at his depth recorder. When the line wavers promisingly, the fisherman rapidly turns the wheel and runs back over the spot to dump his trap, taking into account how wind, tide, waves, and current will affect its ultimate landing place. Every time the trap is pulled, he repositions it according to the catch he is obtaining from the area.

Viewed from the air, some trap strings seem to be laid out in long rows, while others seem to be laid helter-skelter. Placement often distinguishes skilled fishermen from novices. Skilled men try to place traps where they will be productive, regardless of geometry. Novices tend to place long strings where they can keep track of them better. Considerations of precise depth, type of bottom, and so on are of secondary importance to them.

Political factors also influence fishing. A man always places traps in the territory traditional to his harbor gang except in those few instances where he is willing to risk trap losses for political gain. He also has to learn to keep a distance from men in his own gang who have a penchant for trouble or from highliners. Exactly how close a man can crowd a neighbor depends on his own standing in the harbor gang and his relationship to the other person. Moreover, fishermen commonly place traps in areas where they do not expect to catch lobsters simply to reserve the spot for a later time, when they hope that prospects will be better. This "camping out," as it is called, is particularly prevalent in Casco Bay, where an escalation in numbers of traps has led to great trap congestion.

Sometimes fishermen place all their traps on one type of bottom, but normally they fish in more than one ecozone. One day I accompanied a fisherman who placed five strings of traps on the top of subterranean ledges; he placed another thirty traps on other hard bottom, and positioned ten or twelve traps to "scout out the bottom"; another five traps were "camped out" on a spot that would presumably produce in ten days. He moved about a quarter of the traps he pulled during the day to different locations. Most were "thrown over" (placed) within a few hundred yards of their original location, but he took some forty traps three miles farther out to sea to an area where he expected lobsters to migrate shortly.

In placing traps, generalizations count for little. Inexperienced fishermen can sometimes talk with great authority about the way lobsters move and their habits in general, but fishing success depends more strongly on a detailed knowledge of the bottom, a knack for experimentation to find lobster concentrations, and the ability to use these resources effectively. Highly skilled fishermen can not only figure out what to do but also do it. Novices may know that traps placed at eighteen fathoms on the edge of the mud are doing well, but an entirely different skill is required to place traps consistently on that type of bottom.

To reiterate, when placing traps, fishermen take into account a large number of factors to maximize the catch relative to the cost of gasoline, bait, and trap losses. Until I spent a day on a boat with an experienced fisherman who was in the habit of talking to himself, I had not fully appreciated the complexity of trap placement. I was amazed at the number of factors he was considering simultaneously.

Learning Lobstering

In the lobster industry, where secrecy is the rule, most information is obtained by experimentation and relatively little from other fishermen. In the past, knowledge about depths could be learned only by using a hand-line or by noting how much warp was required in a particular place. A fisherman could tell if the bottom was rocky or muddy only by feeling the lead line as it bounced off rocks or sank into soft bottom, or by looking for mud on the traps when they were pulled.

Fishermen formerly learned the bottom using the most rudimentary of navigational equipment. Knowledge about the depth or the bottom in a particular location was worth little unless the man could locate the same spot again. Before the advent of loran C, which allows even relatively inexperienced fishermen to locate themselves within a few yards, some people made maps. In the days before sophisticated electronic gear, most fishermen navigated by reference to objects on shore and by memorizing the pattern of the bottom and other named fishing grounds. Many fishermen still navigate inshore waters this way. I have heard a fisherman describe a place as "a big sand hump," located where an imaginary line, thirty degrees off from the Boothbay dump (located by the column of smoke) intersected another such line marked by a position where one could no longer see any space between Allen Island and Burnt Island. In another case, a fisherman said he was operating about five miles from the mainland, on a line between Chamberlain and Manana Island.

In our own times, the task of learning the bottom and locating certain features is made much simpler by the extensive use of charts, depth finders, depth recorders, and advanced navigational equipment, especially loran C. These aids allow a fisherman not only to see the depth at a glance, but also to identify the type of bottom. Muddy bottom gives off a much weaker echo than rocky bottom.

Though novice fishermen now have an easier time finding the depth and bottom, they still may not have the experience to use that information to reduce trap losses or increase catches. One young fisherman placed a small string of traps in a place where he was sure they were safe, completely unaware that it was a ledge adjoined by much deeper water on the seaward side. He lost the entire string when a storm dragged his traps into the trench.

The better fishermen still memorize good lobstering areas and do not depend on their electronic machinery completely. Not only can they find the larger, well-known areas more rapidly than the unskilled fisherman, they also know about and can relocate relatively small features—a particular mud hole, a small rocky mount, or a long ribbon of edge.

No fisherman can count on doing exactly the same thing from year to year. Highline fishermen experiment constantly with gear, bait, depths, and locations. The most successful fishermen learn to predict where lobsters can be caught by using test traps, pulling a few traps in areas where they believe lobsters have not yet migrated and keeping others behind. When the "rear traps" no longer catch anything but undersized lobsters, and the "lead traps" begin to produce, the fishermen moves the whole string closer to the lead traps. If a fisherman does not pull his traps for a few days, his information becomes dated. One man said, "One time I got sick and didn't pull a trap for three weeks. When I went back to fishing, it took another three weeks to get back on them again. I had just lost the feel of what they were doing."

Fishermen learn a great deal from one another and watch each other like hawks. Some consistently listen in on other men's radio conversations to find out where they are fishing and how they are doing. Some resort to pulling others' traps. Most important, they carefully observe where other fishermen—especially known high-liners—put traps. One man mapped the locations where four or five good fishermen had their gear. Experienced fishermen usually learn such information unobtrusively. Novices are not so subtle. They sometimes follow a highline fisherman and put their traps where he does, almost literally on top of his. Often, remarkably little learning takes place in the process. The novice does not ask *why* the high-liner has placed his traps in this location or notice the pattern of trap movements. He had learned only that the highliner knows how to catch lobsters. Highline fishermen greatly resent these tactics. Not only do the novices' traps invariably get tangled with theirs, but such activities are bound to reduce the catch per trap.

On occasion, an experienced fisherman simply cuts off the traps of a man who has "dumped [traps] on top of him." Ordinarily, however, more subtle means are used to discourage "admirers." A skilled fish-erman may put traps in places he knows are not productive. There are verified stories of experienced men anchoring buoys on pieces of concrete blocks to simulate a string of traps. Sometimes such tactics bring unintended benefits and information. In a small-town store I overheard a not-very-bright local youth loudly announce his discov-ery that "some goddamned fool was fishing a concrete block out in the bay." There was only one way he could have known what was on the end of the buoy, of course. I heard later that he was "punched out" by the "fool," who as one might expect, was one of the best fishermen around. On one occasion, highline lobstermen put strings of traps dangerously close to shore when a storm was brewing, mov-ing them into deeper water at the last minute. Any novices lured into the shallow water by these tactics were certain to lose a few traps. In just this manner, two novice fishermen from an offshore is-land lost strings of traps by dumping on a highline fisherman just before a gale. Still, the rewards of following a highline fisherman are so great that most novices, and even more experienced fishermen, are guilty of the practice at one time or another.

Some of the other ruses employed by highline lobstermen are more elaborate, and more rewarding. One summer in the late 1970s, a good fisherman from Bailey's Island continued to fish in deep water late into the spring when others had concentrated their traps inshore. He knew there were no great numbers of lobsters offshore, but without competition there were still enough to ensure profitability. To keep his find a secret, he would hoist the ordinary white sail on his boat in the morning and fish trap strings placed inshore, talking constantly on the radio to call attention to himself. All afternoon he would separate himself from any boats in the immediate area, raise a colored sail, and fish far outside in deep water. When he returned inshore, he would again raise his white sail and come into the dock to sell his large catch, pretending he had been fishing inshore waters all day long.[4] The secret of his location was also maintained by deceptive banter at the buyers' dock. This fisherman gleefully reported that others used to watch him very carefully and even pulled some of his inshore traps to discover the secret of his inshore catch.

While all lobster fishermen learn by observing one another, by talking to one another, and by direct experience, they depend on these different sources to different degrees. Many able fishermen rely primarily on their own experience, for there are very few people from whom they can learn much. For novice fishermen, the situation is reversed. Since they have little experience to draw on, they must rely on observation.

The Value of Skills

How much are these trap placement skills worth? While our evidence suggests that such skills affect both catches and income, their effect is very difficult to assess. There are two key problems. First, catches are affected by many factors, and the contribution of skill can be assessed only by comparing men of different levels, fishing in the same area and the same season, with the same kind of traps. Second, the degree of skill is hard to document. The cult of secrecy around fishing does not make this task any easier.

In a few instances, we were able to get controlled comparisons so that the effect of skill levels on catches could be accurately measured. During the summer of 1977, we compared catches by a sample of men that key informants identified as high-skilled and medium-skilled from Bremen and New Harbor who were using similar-sized traps. In every case, the more skilled fishermen caught more pounds of lobster per layover day.

However, trap-placement skills appear to have different effects under different circumstances. In New Harbor, high-skilled fishermen, using four-foot traps, caught 0.453 pounds per trap per layover day, while medium-skilled fishermen, using similar traps, caught only 0.174 pounds—less than half as much per unit of effort. In the same season, however, the same high-skilled fishermen caught only 4 percent more lobsters per layover day than less skilled fishermen when they were using three-foot traps. The reasons for this are not known with any certainty. One can conclude only that under certain circumstances, trap-placement skills seem to produce excellent results; under others, they produce only marginal increases in catches. But in all cases, they improve catches. These results are strongly reinforced by a regression analysis of our 1978 catch data on factors influencing lobster catches. This analysis also leads to the conclusion that trap-placement skills make a substantial difference in catches (Acheson 1980b: 20–22).

Nothing about income can be gleaned from these data. In an earlier study (1972–73), however, we gathered information from a small sample of fishermen in the same area concerning the effect of trap-placement skills on income. The men who placed their traps with pinpoint accuracy had a gross income from lobstering of $18,640, while those who saturated the bay with their gear grossed only $14,555 from lobster fishing, a difference of $4,085. Although only thirty-three fishermen were involved in this study, the 28 percent difference in mean income is statistically significant (Acheson 1977: 130). But these results need to be taken with more than a grain of salt. Some of the verbal reports on income seem dubious. Moreover, this study was relatively unsophisticated in that no data were collected on bait, trap length, trap type, fishing effort, or many other factors that we have since learned affect catches. It is uncertain, therefore, how much of the difference in income is due to differences in trap-placement skills and how much to other practices. For whatever it is worth, skilled fishermen say that such skills can mean several thousand dollars to an individual who is fortunate enough to have them.

Incomes earned in the fishery range widely. In the mid 1980s some full-time fishermen earned less than $7000 after taxes and expenses were paid, while another paid income taxes on $46,000—almost all from lobstering. The disposable income of the average fisherman working full-time for at least seven months a year is about $22,000. A hard-driving, skilled lobsterman with a big gang of traps might have a disposable income of some $35,000 from the fishery.

Innovation

In the long run, the most important decisions a fisherman must make concern the species for which he will fish and the kind of boat and gear he will use. The two decisions are closely connected, since a limited repertoire of gear can be used to catch any given type of fish.

The Maine lobster industry has not undergone the same kind of technical revolution that has occurred in other industries. Lobsters have always been caught in traps very similar to those in use today. The adoption of the internal combustion engine around 1885–1910 was perhaps the single most important innovation to occur in the lobster industry in the past century. Motors, which made sails obsolete, greatly increased the range of boats, increased maneuverability, and forced changes in hull design (Lunt 1975). In the past thirty-five years, very few innovations have been accepted by the industry in general, and even fewer represent any radical change. The 1960s saw the widespread adoption of hydraulic haulers and citizen's band radios, but even these had antecedents in the donkey engines (auxiliary trap-hauling engines) and winches used since World War I, and in the single sideband radios used since the early 1940s. The late 1960s and early 1970s saw hemp rope and wooden buoys replaced by artificial rope and Styrofoam.

The introduction of metal traps during the late 1970s and early 1980s afforded a chance to study the factors promoting technical change in the Maine lobster industry. In 1977, when metal traps were first being introduced, some experienced fishermen were sure that they worked well and planned to buy many; others thought that they were not worth the money. In order to study the factors behind the adoption of metal traps, we gathered data for over a year and a half from fishermen in Pemaquid Harbor, New Harbor, Bremen, and Friendship concerning the catches of various kinds of traps and the characteristics of the men who were adopting or not adopting them. As noted earlier, analysis of the catch data showed that aluminized wire traps caught more lobsters per unit of effort than did vinyl traps in general and that both kinds of metal traps outfished wooden traps. Certainly the metal traps were worth the increased purchase price (Acheson 1982: 290–98). But because these facts were not widely appreciated in the late 1970s, a willingness to adopt metal traps depended on a number of social factors, including a fisherman's harbor gang and his position in that gang.

When metal traps first began to diffuse in the midcoastal region, information about them was clearly restricted and managed by the men who had adopted them. At that time, fishermen frequently claimed that there was no difference in catches. Ostensibly people adopted them only to avoid the worm problem (marine worms can destroy wooden traps) and to ease their work load, since metal traps are lighter and easier to handle out of water. These reasons are valid, but they mask the fact that many owners of metal traps felt that they fished better. By the fall of 1978, many lobstermen began to suspect the truth. At that time another verbal ploy was tried. Knowledgeable fishermen began to talk about "metal traps," as if there were no difference between aluminized and vinyl-covered wire traps. Gradually, reasonably accurate information about the catches of various kinds of traps spread throughout the region, but the situation was confused for at least a year and a half—even in harbor gangs where metal traps had been accepted by some men relatively early.

Given the confusion and misinformation, how did fishermen decide to adopt or reject aluminized and vinyl-covered traps? The response to metal traps came far earlier in some harbors than in others. In 1977, they were being used only in the areas around Portland, Stonington, and Muscongus Bay. Moreover, information about metal traps spread very slowly from one harbor to another, undoubtedly because of the hostility and lack of communication between men from different harbors. In 1977, metal traps were being accepted in numbers in Bremen; it took five years for this innovation to find its way to Pemaquid, a distance of only sixteen miles.

Once metal traps were introduced into a harbor gang, they spread throughout the gang relatively fast, though no fishermen interviewed switched completely from wooden to metal traps all at once. They typically bought a few traps and then gradually increased the proportion of metal traps they used.

Moreover, even within each harbor gang, some men adopted metal traps far earlier than others. Acceptance proceeded according to the classic S-shaped curve of innovation (Rogers and Shoemaker 1971: 176–191).[5] On the whole, the early adopters of metal traps (both aluminized and vinyl) were successful fishermen at the zenith of their lobstering careers. Many were highline fishermen in their thirties and early forties. These men had early access to accurate information about metal traps because of their relatively high position in their harbor gang hierarchies. In addition, they were highly competitive men accustomed to trying out innovations in an effort to maintain their position. They had high incomes that allowed them to invest heavily in successful innovations (Acheson 1982b: 300–301). The late adopters were less successful fishermen who were either past their primes or very young. They had far less information about metal traps and their low incomes made the cheaper wooden traps appear to be a better buy.

Switching Fisheries

One of the primary adaptive strategies among fishermen is to shift target species as prices and availability change. The ability to make such shifts often spells the economic difference between success and failure. Changes are so numerous and so frequent that the composition of the fleet changes monthly. Switching fisheries is a complicated process. Maine has more than a dozen major commercial species, a wide variety of boats, many possible combinations of gear and electronic equipment, and thousands of fishermen, each of whom has a unique operation. Though some gear changes are relatively easy, others are more difficult, since they require different boats, different skills, and different levels of investment.[6]

Fisheries can be combined in a number of ways over the annual cycle. Lobstermen commonly combine shrimping or scalloping with their lobstering and may also fish for groundfish using gill nets. These species can be pursued when lobstering is bad and do not require a different boat. The men fish for lobsters in the summer and fall months, switching to scallops or shrimp in midwinter and groundfish in the spring. A few lobster fishermen, especially in the eastern part of the state, operate herring weirs and stop seines on a part-time basis during the summer. They spend their days lobster fishing and their early evening hours checking their herring nets. Along the western coast some lobster fishermen go groundfishing in the spring.

The number of men who combine or switch fisheries varies from year to year. In 1978, 25 percent of the total 2,205 full-time lobster fishermen in Maine switched to another fishery for some part of the annual round (Acheson et al. 1980: table 13). Of the 541 men who switched fisheries, 51 percent went scalloping part of the year; another 28 percent went groundfishing; and 13 percent went fishing for herring. Smaller numbers went swordfishing and clamming. In other years, even more lobstermen switched to other fisheries. When concentrations of shrimp appear off the coast, as they did in the early 1970s and mid 1980s, hundreds of lobstermen switch to shrimp during the winter. In 1985, an estimated 50 percent of the lobster fleet in the midcoastal region was engaged in one or another ancillary fishery over the course of the year. The highest percentage combined lobstering and shrimping, followed by lobstering and groundfishing.

Permanent Changes in Fisheries

It is difficult to generalize about switching fisheries because it is such a complicated phenomenon, given the numerous types of gear, boats, and species involved. We do, however, know a great deal about the kinds of changes that were taking place in the late 1970s and the reasons for those changes.

In our study of captains in Maine and New Hampshire, we obtained data on the primary gear 190 men used in 1973 and in 1978 (Acheson 1980a). In that five-year period, a large number of these fishermen changed the primary type of gear they used and, in most cases, the primary species they caught. The changes in gear are summarized in figure 5.

The data show several different statistically significant trends in gear change. The most important shift observed was from lobster fishing to other fisheries. While 67 of the 190 interviewees switched from lobster to other species as a primary target species, only 2 entered lobster fishing. Twenty-four men changed from lobstering to bottom trawling for groundfish, but only 2 switched the other way. Twenty men changed from lobster fishing to gillnetting for groundfish, and none went the other way. Smaller numbers of lobster fishermen went to longlines, dredges, and stop seines; even smaller numbers changed to purse seines and midwater trawls. None of the longliners, dredge fishermen, seiners, or midwater trawlers switched into lobstering. There was a significant shift from dredge fishing to bottom trawls and gillnets, and from gillnets to bottom trawls.

The late 1970s and early 1980s were characterized by a move away from lobstering, scalloping, and a few other industries and a massive buildup in the groundfishery, as indicated by the number of groundfish licenses granted from the National Marine Fisheries Service in New England. In 1977, 1,200 licenses were issued, while in 1979, the number had increased to 2,191—an 83 percent increase in two years. Given that groundfishing boats are generally larger than lobstering vessels and demand more electronic gear, it is scarcely surprising that in this period the average boat size increased and that more electronic gear was being used on these vessels (Acheson 1984: 322–25).

A primary reason for this shift was that opportunities in groundfishing were expanding while those in lobstering were contracting. In 1973, the total value of Maine lobster landings was 23.2 million dollars; in 1980, the value was 41.7 million dollars, an increase of

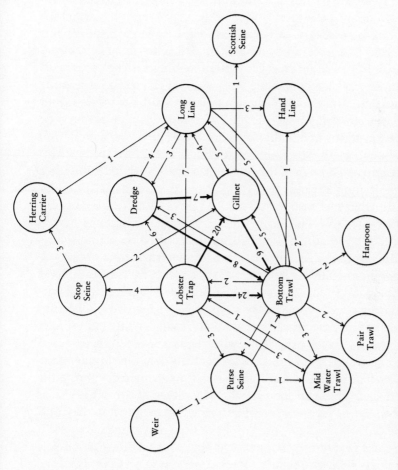

Figure 5. Primary Fishing Gear Changes in Northern New England, 1973–78. One hundred ninety fishermen were studied. Heavy lines indicate statistically significant changes (Acheson 1980a: 466–70).

44 percent. However, inflation was so great that the gross income actually decreased in real dollars. Compounding the problems of lobster fishermen were the rapid cost increases for bait, fuel, and boats. Many lobster fishermen at that time reported real financial difficulties. In 1980, many of the best lobster fishermen had no more purchasing power than they had in 1973. Many said they were experiencing a decline in real income.

At the same time, the catch and value of groundfish increased substantially. In 1973, the total landed value of six common groundfish species was $1.6 million; in 1980, it had increased to $18.5 million, a phenomenal 844 percent rise in real dollars (Acheson 1984: table 7).

The shift from scallop dredges to groundfishing with bottom trawls and gillnets was also connected with relative changes in economic opportunities. Almost all of the boats using scallop dredges in our sample were owned by men from the eastern part of Maine who combine lobstering and scalloping. Neither industry was doing well by 1977—especially since the scallop beds were beginning to become depleted. These men, therefore, changed to groundfishing as a more stable and profitable fishery.

Not all fishermen responded to the changes in fishing opportunities. Most of Maine's full-time lobster fishermen remained in lobstering. Our 1978 study of 190 fishermen turned up a few factors that influenced the decision to switch gears permanently.

Skill and experience play such a critical role in fishing success that men do not suddenly give up gear they have been using and take on equipment with which they have no experience of familiarity (Acheson 1977). Virtually all of those who made changes in primary fishing gear had some experience with the new gear. In many cases, change in primary gear is a precursor of changes in the annual round. Men may first use new gear for a few weeks or months during the year and then gradually increase the percentage of time that gear is used until it has become the primary gear. In the process they may drop the old primary gear completely, or they may continue to use it as secondary gear during part of the annual cycle. Among captains of fishing boats who switched to new primary gear between 1973 and 1978, only seven of the ninety-nine informants on whom we have information had no experience with that gear before using it on their current boats. The majority of the lobstermen who switched gear obtained their experience with the new equipment by using it during part of the year on their own boats, although substantial numbers obtained experience working on boats owned by other people (Acheson 1980a: table 8).

Decisions to enter groundfishing from lobstering were also influenced by the amount of capital needed. Schoolboys enter lobster fishing by the hundreds, with only a few hundred dollars worth of traps and an outboard-powered skiff. Gillnets and stop seines require more capital equipment, and such techniques as pair trawling, purse seining, and offshore beam trawling require vessels between 60 and 100 feet long, worth up to a million dollars, and manned by crews of four to eight.

Some men enter a fishery and remain in it throughout their careers. Most fishermen in Maine and New Hampshire begin their careers as teenagers by going lobstering in skiffs. In their early twenties, most of these boys buy inboard-powered fishing boats and begin to build up large gangs of lobster traps; others may decide to enter different fisheries at this point. Whether they choose finfishing or lobstering, their operation typically reaches its maximum size when they are in their thirties and early forties. By their late forties and early fifties, these fishermen typically begin to reduce their effort and scale of operation. Many finfishermen sell their large boats and return to lobster fishing, ending their careers as they began—lobster fishing from a skiff with a small gang of traps.

These patterns appear to be normal but many variations occur in career paths. Many men switch in and out of fishing and nonfishing jobs as whim and opportunity dictate. During the period of our study, the late 1970s, older men as well as fishermen in their early twenties were moving from lobstering to finfishing. The older men who chose finfishing tended to adopt gillnets, which can easily be combined with lobstering because they can be placed on lobster boats over thirty-five feet long for an investment of less than ten thousand dollars. These senior fishermen favored gillnets because they wished to remain essentially in lobstering and did not want to invest in larger boats and additional gear, especially since this change would necessitate spending greater amounts of time away from home. Men in their twenties or early thirties who decided to switch from lobstering, or a combination of lobster fishing and dragging, usually chose to groundfish with bottom trawls. If this type of fishing demanded greater investment and more time away from home, it also promised a higher income. The mean age of men who adopted bottom trawls was 32.7 years, and of men who adopted gillnets, 38.0 years. This difference is significant at the .01 level (Acheson 1980a: 474).

Access to markets also influenced the move from lobstering to groundfishing. Only seventeen ports in Maine have groundfish dealers, and the men who adopted groundfish gear were located in or near those ports.

Finally, the ability to get substantial amounts of credit allowed some lobster fishermen to enter such fisheries as bottom trawling, which require a larger vessel. Much of the money for the new boats and equipment came from the Farm Credit Service. Several lobster fishermen who wanted to enter groundfishing did not have the kind of business track record required for loans from the service and were forced to remain in the lobster industry.

The kinds of factors at work are probably unique in each shift of fishery. For example, in a change from lobstering to groundfishing, the ability to obtain large amounts of capital, proximity to groundfish dealers, experience in using groundfish gear, age of the fisherman, and related career-cycle factors were all critical in influencing the decisions to switch. If the switch had been in the opposite direction, none of these variables would have been of key importance. The typical groundfisherman could sell his dragger, buy a lobster boat, and have money left over; there are lobster dealers and cooperatives in every harbor; almost every fisherman has some experience lobstering; and age is no obstacle to entering the lobster fishery. However, the lobster fishery is strongly territorial, whereas no territories exist for groundfishermen; those making the switch into lobstering would have to take this factor into account.

1. Wooden traps being loaded aboard a lobster boat in Casco Bay. Traps are brought ashore and stored on docks or on land during the slow seasons in the annual cycle (late winter and again during the early summer shedding season). This procedure kills all the sea growth on them. They are then loaded on boats and repositioned in early spring and again in July. (Courtesy of *The Times Record*, Brunswick, Maine).

2. A lobster fisherman leaves the dock with a small load of traps. (Courtesy of *The Times Record*, Brunswick, Maine).

3. A lobster boat in Muscongus Bay. Flocks of sea gulls often follow boats to get the used bait that is taken from traps and thrown overboard. At two or three miles distance, boats would be almost invisible if it were not for the swarms of gulls circling overhead.

4. Brian Sawyer, a highline fisherman, heads out of New Harbor and begins searching the waters ahead for his first string of traps.

5. Dan Cheney, a fisherman and pound owner from Pemaquid Harbor, measures lobsters from his catch at the dock. To be legal in 1987, the lobster had to be between 3 3/16 inches and 5 inches on the carapace (measured from the eye socket to the back of the body). These brass gauges are made according to specifications set by Maine law.

6. A berried, notch-tailed lobster. Eggs glued to her abdomen and a notch cut in her tail, in the second flipper from the left, are visible. Although the notch has grown in partially, it indicates to fishermen who catch this lobster when it is not bearing eggs that it forms part of the breeding stock. Notch-tailed lobsters are always returned to the water.

7. Charlie Begin, Boothbay Harbor, pulls a three-foot wooden trap over the rail. The hydraulic hauler is pulling up the second trap in the string. (Note the taut warp line over the snatch block.) Squirrel Island is in the background.

8. Fred Schopfer, sternman on Charlie Begin's boat, loads a baiting iron with redfish frames. The redfish are placed in the trap by putting the end of the bait string, attached to the trap bottom, through the hold in the end of the baiting iron. The fish are then pushed onto the string.

9. Gardiner Gross from Deer Isle and his sternman, Calvin, wait for another trap to come over the side of the boat.

10. Fred Schopfer loads herring into a bait bag. This picture was taken just before dawn in an early November snow squall.

11. Ed Drisko, who has done as much as anyone to introduce the author to the intricacies of lobster fishing, unloads his catch at the New Harbor Cooperative. The crate in the foreground holds about a hundred pounds of lobsters. Once packed, these crates are submerged under floating docks, called "cars." The lobsters are thus kept alive but packed for shipment. Note the rubber bands on the lobster's claws to prevent fighting and cannibalism.

12. A crate of lobsters being pulled from a car in Friendship. The scale at the right is used for weighing the crates.

13. Shooting the breeze at the Keene Narrows Lobster Pound in Bremen.

14. Lobster buoys washed ashore at Pemquid beach. These buoys may have been cut off by passing boats, but it is more likely that they were cut off in a small-scale dispute over lobstering territory in John's Bay.

15. Kendall Winchenback, Friendship, dipnets herring he has purchased from a dealer for use the following day as bait. In recent years, herring has become the primary bait in the lobster fishery.

16. Woodbury Post and his son bring fishing gear down to the dock at Spruce Head Lobster Cooperative. The Post family fishes a perimeter-defended area around Metinic Island, which they have owned for generations. Woody stays in a house on the island during the summer and must ferry all the fishing gear, bait, food, and fuel to the island himself. Staying on the island, however, saves a two-hour boat trip every day.

17. Wire lobster traps on a dock at Boothbay during June—the shedding season. Such scenes give some idea of the large numbers of traps currently used by fishermen, especially in the areas where trawl fishing is allowed.

18. Bill Barter, manager of a lobster pound in Hancock, places a crate of lobsters in a car.

19. Weighing and packing lobsters at the Lusty Lobster Company in Bremen. Lobsters are placed in cardboard cartons packed with seaweed and ice for shipment to other parts of the world.

20. While few women go lobster fishing at present, many help with the shoreside aspects of the business by keeping the books, arranging for maintenance, and tending to other business matters. Cindy Brackett takes a more active role than most. She runs the Captain's Catch restaurant and retail store at Pemaquid Beach. The menu features lobsters and crabs caught mostly by her husband, Steve. Here she is selling lobsters to a retail customer. At the right is the cooker, which is heated by a standard oil furnace gun. At the left is a running seawater tank for the lobsters.

21. Eddie Blackmore (with seagull tie), president of the Maine Lobstermen's Association, talks with fishermen at the Maine Fisherman's Forum in Rockland.

22. A modest house with a small number of new wire traps at Pemaquid Falls.

23. Maynard Winchenback inside his shop at the Wallace Shellfish Company in Friendship. Several fishermen who have been selling their catches to the company for many years are allowed to use small shops there, where they can build traps and store equipment. During the slow winter months, these shops become club houses, where men alternate between building gear, telling stories, visiting, and an occasional game of cards.

CHAPTER 6

Markets

The ties that lobster fishermen have with dealers and others in the marketing chain are of critical importance. As we shall see, they lower uncertainty for both the fishermen and the dealers in several different ways.

Lobsters from Maine docks are distributed throughout the world by means of a complicated network of dealers, pounds, wholesale firms, shippers, and retailers. Most seafood sold in the United States goes to the institutional trade. It is estimated that at least 70 percent of all lobsters are eaten in restaurants, hotels, clubs, or other institutions, although an increasing number is being sold to supermarket chains for individual consumption.

Between the fishermen and the consumer are several kinds of middlemen. Dozens of small wholesale and retail operations buy lobsters from dealers and cooperatives. More than thirty lobster pounds, with an estimated capacity of 2.5 million pounds, operate in Maine. In the summer and early fall, when catches are high and prices are low, the operators of these pounds buy lobsters from Maine and Canadian dealers, cooperatives, and fishermen, then sell them in the winter to take advantage of the substantial rise in price. Some pound operators also buy smaller amounts of lobster during the spring spurt and sell them to tourists by early July, when catches fall off because of shedding. Some pounds are run and managed by their owners; others are leased to wholesale firms.

Numerous small trucking operations buy lobsters from dealers and cooperatives and sell them in the larger cities along the East Coast. Many companies have only one or two trucks and a couple of employees. Three large, vertically integrated firms own dealerships, pounds, and wholesaling houses, and handle millions of pounds of lobster in both New England and Canada. James Hook, A. M. Look, and Bay State Lobster all maintain their headquarters and wholesale operations in Boston and ship to all parts of the globe.

Other distribution firms are scattered all over the nation, as well as in Europe and Japan. Seafood wholesale firms located in major cities buy large amounts of lobsters from wholesalers in New England and sell to fish stores, restaurants, supermarket chains, and other outlets in their own areas. Very little information is available on the distribution system in Europe or Japan.

An estimated 70 percent of the lobsters caught by Maine fishermen is purchased by one of the seventeen cooperatives or eighty-five dealers that sell mostly to wholesalers. In the summer, however, up to 30 percent of the lobsters bought by an average dealership or cooperative might be sold to retail customers. A few dealers and co-ops run restaurants on the docks. Large quantities are sold also to local stores and restaurants. In the cold months of the year, when tourists are scarce, most of the catch finds its way to more distant distributors.

A much smaller amount of lobster is sold by fishermen directly. In the summer, on the southern part of the Maine coast and especially in the Portland area, where there are many restaurants, hotels, and fish stores, fishermen sell about 20 percent of the catch to consumers. In eastern Maine, where there are fewer tourists, only an estimated 10 percent is sold directly.

An estimated 25 percent of the total Maine catch is handled by the three large, vertically integrated firms. In the recent past, Hook, Look, and Bay State may have handled a higher proportion of the state's catch, but according to most reports, their proportion has dropped in recent years. A smaller proportion is purchased by small, independent truckers, who buy a few thousand pounds of lobsters at a time for shipment to cities in the Northeast.

The operations of all of the firms in the marketing chain vary enormously. Firms combine different types of business, buy lobsters in different places, sell them in different places, and sell different amounts through diverse channels. For example, the Swans Island Cooperative sells all its lobsters to two wholesalers. It does not handle groundfish, nor does it retail a lot of lobsters. The nearby Stonington Cooperative operates as a combined cooperative and wholesale house. It sells most of its lobsters to distributors and chains in the United States and Europe. It also does a sizable retail business. One dealership on the Pemaquid peninsula buys lobsters from only a few fishermen and makes most of its money on a restaurant operation; another sells a large percentage of its lobsters retail. Still a third has no retail or restaurant operation at all but runs a very large pound. Some of these firms seem to make little sense from an operational standpoint. One Boston-based firm, a few miles from Logan International Airport, trucks most of its lobsters to New York and other cities in the Northeast. Meanwhile, Graffam Brothers in Rockport, Maine—about seventy miles from Bangor International Airport—airfreights a high proportion of its lobsters all over the world.

An expanded lobster market is the result of improved transportation. Until the 1930s, lobsters were shipped by boats equipped with circulating seawater tanks. In effect, this technology limited the live lobster market to the cities of the Northeast. Modern refrigeration techniques and airfreight have greatly increased the range over which lobsters can be marketed, but even now there are limits. Properly iced and packed, soft-shelled lobster can be kept out of water for about twenty-four hours and hard-shelled lobsters for about forty-eight hours with no more than 10 percent mortality. If the destination is within a thousand miles, the lobsters can be transported by truck; if the shipment is for Europe or the West Coast, they must go by plane. Most wholesalers prefer to use trucks, if they own any, whenever distance permits. Transportation by truck is cheaper and prevents collection problems, since the driver can be instructed to get payment on the spot.

Several factors combine to make the marketing of lobsters a risky and uncertain business. First, as at sea, secrecy reigns in the market. Loose talk about sources of supply or markets may lead to increased

competition and reduce the chances for negotiating the best agreements possible. As a result, dealers and wholesalers give little information about prices and supplies. Second, large price changes can
occur unpredictably. Although there is a cyclical pattern in prices
and catches, even short-term prices are impossible to predict. A fisherman can leave in the morning expecting a particular price, only to
find out that the price has changed twenty or thirty cents by the
time he lands his catch in the evening. Everyone in the industry is
aware that the highest price of the year is paid in the winter, but no
one is sure when the price will peak or what the best price will be.
Lobsters are more plentiful in some years than in others. In the summer of 1984, lobsters were so scarce that fishermen were predicting
the collapse of the whole industry. In the summer of 1985, lobsters
were so abundant that everyone was complaining about the bottom
dropping out of the market.

Sharp business practices are characteristic of the lobster market.
Outright lying and cheating are certainly less frequent today than in
the past, in great measure because of the formation of cooperatives.
Dealers and wholesalers, however, tend to use their differential
knowledge of markets to their own advantage. They commonly delay a price increase as long as possible, though eventually they must
pay the increase or face the prospect of losing business because the
fishermen go elsewhere. One dealer pointed out that if he could
avoid giving a five-cent increase for a week, he would make eight
hundred dollars. He succumbed to that temptation for the week and
a half it took his fishermen to figure it out.

Relationships along the Marketing Chain

The number of firms with which a wholesaler or dealer has steady
ties varies. It is not unusual for some small dealers to sell most of
their lobsters to one wholesaling firm; small wholesale houses may
sell most of their lobsters to three to five customers. The larger
wholesale and retail firms buy and sell to more firms, although the
number with which they regularly do business remains relatively
small.

These firms usually have informal understandings that they will do business with one another in the long run. Prices are negotiated based on the going rate for the time of year. Such agreements are of critical importance in ameliorating some pressing problems faced by everyone in the marketing chain: how to get enough lobsters in times of scarcity (such as midsummer and winter), how to satisfy customers, and how to find markets for the overabundance in the fall months.

Dealers and wholesalers are caught between the expectations of fishermen and those of consumers. The fisherman demands to be paid on the day of the catch, regardless of how many or how few lobsters he brings in. Restaurants, hotels, and other institutions ordinarily want a steady supply of lobsters, and they prefer to charge a steady price—in part because of a reluctance to reprint menus. If dealers do not buy lobsters from fishermen during times of glut, or do not supply their customers in times of scarcity, their fishermen and customers will seek out other dealers and wholesalers.

The strong, bilateral ties between firms in the marketing chain go a long way toward solving this problem. In times of scarcity, wholesalers know that the dealers with whom they have ties will do their best to supply them; dealers know that in times of glut, their wholesalers will relieve them of as many lobsters as possible. In the words of one dealer, "It don't guarantee nothing; they just mean you get first preference. If the man is going to buy or sell to anyone, it will be with you if he possibly can." Firms with long-term bilateral ties know that the terms of an agreement will be kept. Delivery schedules will be fulfilled, and payment will be prompt. These ties are clearly worth much to dealers and wholesalers, who are willing to forgo short-run financial gain to maintain them.

The importance of bilateral agreements between buyers and sellers was brought home to me during a conversation with a pound operator who sells almost all of his lobsters to a wholesaler in Portland. I asked, "Would you sell five thousand pounds of your lobsters to a trucker you didn't know, if he offered you twenty cents over the going price per pound?" He replied, "I wouldn't do it. My wholesaler is counting on these lobsters, and if he doesn't get them, he'll find another source of supply. I have a good working relationship with him, and I wouldn't jeopardize that for a few hundred dollars. Besides, I wouldn't know for two weeks if his check [the trucker's] was good."

At the same time, there is a good deal of suspicion and some hostility among firms up and down the marketing chain. Once made, most agreements are carried out faithfully, but in the negotiations a firm always looks out for its own interest. Firms that buy and sell lobsters to each other are mutually dependent; yet their interests, particularly in prices, are not coincident by any means. People can never count on accurate price information. There is probably a good deal of truth in the statement of the dealer who said, "They will take you if they can. Your only protection is to know who you are dealing with. Even then you have to look out." Dealers and wholesalers often describe their relationships in terms of hostility mixed with humor. When these men talk to each other on the phone or in person, their gruff, sharp comments may mask considerable respect, even affection, or may be as hostile as they sound.

Firms in the same locality at the same level of the marketing chain have a very different but no less essential relationship with one another. Even competitors for the same customers and sources of supply are often very cooperative and dependent on one another for accurate information. The price information they provide one another is often more accurate than information from the people with whom they buy and sell. Dealers and co-op managers in an area all know one another and are part of a dense network. They are constantly on the phone about prices, sources of bait, fuel, and so on. In a similar fashion, the wholesale and retail firms in any city all know one another and regularly exchange information. The Portland and Boston dealers, as one man expressed it, "all have their heads together," and the same could be said about the people in the Fulton Fish Market in New York. Often, more tangible assets are exchanged. Dealers and managers of cooperatives in a local area frequently sell bait and lend equipment to one another.

Relationships between any two nearby dealers or wholesalers vary considerably. Bitter enmity, which usually has its roots in faulty information or taking over markets or sources of supply belonging to another, sometimes exists. Others are very friendly. When one wholesaler's dock and establishment burned, he was able to move in with another wholesaler, an old friend. They shared the same office and conducted business from two desks on opposite sides of the room. The burned-out wholesaler also used some of his friend's storage tanks to store his lobsters. Fishermen were surprised and intrigued to see two "competitors" making deals and talking on the phone about confidential matters within earshot of each other. One of them explained, "I don't steal his customers and he doesn't take mine. We can get along fine in the same office."

Usually the relationship between nearby dealers and wholesalers is a mixture of cooperation and competition. The complex nature of the relationship between nearby firms at the same market level is revealed in conversations that mix friendly jokes and accurate information with barbed commentary and deceptive data. It is not uncommon for dealers to have little interaction with their closest competitors, but they do take care to cultivate relationships with others in the same area and the same segment of the industry. One dealer stated it this way: "Perhaps you might never speak to the dealer across the harbor. He is the real competition because he can take your fishermen, but you would know a dealer or two in the next harbor up and perhaps the nearest co-op manager."

Fishermen and dealers also enter into long-term arrangements to reduce risk. Their relationships are more ambivalent, and exchanges between them are different from those between dealers, wholesalers, and others in the marketing chain. While fishermen are very dependent on their dealers, the relationships are tinged with suspicion and hostility. Many fishermen are convinced that dealers are in a conspiracy to cheat them. Fishermen usually agree to sell all or most of their catch to "the man they fish for." The dealer, for his part, gives the fisherman several things in return. Perhaps most important, a dealer gives his fishermen a steady, secure market. Dealers buy all the lobsters their fishermen offer for sale, regardless of how glutted the market might be. The dealer supplies his fishermen with gasoline, diesel fuel, gloves, paint, buoys, and bait at cost or with only a small markup. Supplying bait is the dealers' biggest problem because it is a critical item and supplies are irregular. A dealer normally allows his fishermen to use his dock free of charge, a service that is worth a lot in a region where the cost of coastal land has risen astronomically.

The precise deal between a fisherman and a dealer is individually negotiated. The willingness of the dealer to give extra concessions to a particular fisherman depends in part on the length of time they have been doing business and the amount of trust built up between them. Some fishermen have been able to obtain workshop or storage space. Others have arranged for preferential access to bait in times of shortage. Sometimes dealers offer selected fishermen interest-free loans for boats, equipment, and traps. Usually such loans are given only with the proviso that the fishermen continue to do business with the dealer. As repayment dealers often take a percentage of each day's catch. In a few cases dealers have even given some of their fishermen slightly higher prices for their catches. Ordinarily, such special deals are kept as secret as possible. Special deals and loans may also be given to fishermen when the dealer wants to increase the number of fishermen doing business with him.

Fishermen and dealers gain different things in their exchanges with each other. The dealer wants to secure a large and reliable supply of lobsters to satisfy customers who will go elsewhere if their orders are unfilled. Since there is little price competition, the primary way for dealers to obtain a steady supply of lobsters is to attach as many fishermen to their firms as possible. From this perspective, low-cost gas and bait, dock space, and loans are exchanged for a reliable source of lobsters.

By agreeing to sell their lobsters to a dealer at the established price, fishermen are in essence agreeing to give up the right to bargain in exchange for loans, bait, gas, dock space, and a sure market. Why do they forfeit the right to bargain with an untrustworthy dealer? The fact is that lobster fishermen are not in a good bargaining position. The dealer has more information, and it makes little sense for them to try to outwit the dealer by scheduling their fishing activities when the price is highest. In short, agreeing to sell to a single dealer is a rational strategy. By giving up an already weak ability to bargain, fishermen exchange something that has little practical value for things of solid worth.

Although fishermen compete for lobsters and territory, they do exchange accurate information about prices. Most of the information is exchanged within harbor gangs, although fishermen do check with men from other harbors. If fishermen feel that they should get a higher price, they sometimes complain to their dealers, either singly or in small groups. Such discussions can become unfriendly at times.

Negotiating Prices

Dealers and cooperative managers usually contact each other daily to exchange information and speculate on impending price changes, supplies of lobsters, and the state of the market. The price for which the dealer or cooperative manager sells lobsters to wholesalers is based on the "boat price," the rate given to fishermen. A normal markup in 1984 was thirty to thirty-five cents per pound over the boat price, and this is what most dealers and managers try to get from their wholesalers. Wholesalers also set the selling price in terms of a fixed increase over buying price. The exact price depends in great part on how far away the customer is and the type of services the wholesaler provides. If wholesalers are providing storage tanks or must ship long distances, they charge more.

Dealers and wholesalers feel pressured to pay the same prices as any others in the area. If a dealer pays his fishermen more than other dealers, he often cannot pass on his increased costs to the firms to which he sells, since they can obtain cheaper lobsters elsewhere. If he pays a lower price than other dealers and co-op managers in an area, his fishermen may become angry and switch dealers entirely. What can happen when one dealer or wholesaler does not keep his prices in line with those around him is exemplified in the history of the Boothbay Cooperative. When the cooperative first started in 1971, the manager deliberately raised the boat price fifty cents per pound over the going price to help his fishermen. Fishermen from all over the region swarmed to sell, and other dealers in the area stopped buying lobsters. At the end of two weeks, the Boothbay Cooperative discovered that it could not pass on the increase to wholesalers, who were buying large amounts of lobster elsewhere in the state. The co-op manager found himself with dozens of fishermen expecting him to buy their lobsters at a premium, but he had no market for them. Within a few days the co-op lowered its price again. Many fishermen in the region believed that the co-op's loss was due to collusion among the dealers and wholesalers. Nevertheless, it became clear that financial problems followed when lobster prices were not kept in line with those of nearby competitors.

Dealers on the same peninsula thus usually pay a price identical with, or within ten cents of, what others are paying. Along the entire coast, the variation in boat price is usually less than twenty-five cents. Cooperatives pay their members not only when lobsters are being sold, but also in a bonus at the end of the year. The boat prices paid by cooperatives are more variable, but they are comparable to those of private dealers when the year-end bonus is included.

Price changes are negotiated between firms in the marketing chain, always with a view to what other firms are doing and to supply and demand. When lobster catches are high in the fall, wholesalers and distributors cannot sell all of the lobsters. They offer lower prices or stop buying entirely in order to get rid of the catch. As noted earlier, much of the catch at this time is bought up by pound operators. In times of scarcity, dealers and distributors bid up the price of lobster. If they are desperate for lobster and face the prospect of losing valuable customers, dealers sometimes offer sharply higher prices as an inducement to fishermen to sell to them instead of to other dealers.

Negotiations among dealers, wholesalers, and retailers resemble a delicate dance. Owners of firms seek to drive as hard a bargain as possible and still maintain long-term relationships with suppliers and buyers. Individuals commonly withhold information from those with whom they do business in an effort to strengthen their negotiating positions. Bluffing and deception, not to say outright lying, are not uncommon. Yet a man does not want to be caught in too many falsehoods or appear to be applying continual pressure for price changes on firms up and down the marketing chain, for fear that valued relationships may be severed. Men commonly assert that they are merely following the market—for example, that someone else is already buying lobsters at the desired price or is willing to sell them at that price. This ploy works because everyone in the industry knows the importance of being in line with the market.

Often several dealers or wholesalers in a city agree to hold out for a higher price, hoping that they can do jointly what one person cannot. If all change price at once, the onus is spread, the sellers avoid angering long-term trading partners, and they also send a powerful message about changing market conditions. One small dealer said, "I try to build the price around me," meaning that he tries to get other dealers, pound operators, and co-op managers to change prices simultaneously or even a little ahead of him. Though some dealers and others in the marketing chain do very little negotiating—they simply make a few phone calls in the morning to find out the boat price and buy and sell accordingly—most do negotiate, and some do so constantly.

Negotiating a new price, dealers and wholesalers insist, is an uncertain business, especially when they have to negotiate a price days in advance of actual delivery. A Portland dealer who supplies a chain of stores in a distant state usually negotiates price about ten days in advance. He says, "All I have to go on is my sense of where the market is headed. If I quote a price and the actual price of lobster goes up, I lose money; if it goes down, I make more than I planned. Sometimes you gain and sometimes you lose on these deals." Successful negotiating depends to a large degree on information that is costly and difficult to obtain.

To get the Boston price, many people use the *Boston Blue Sheet*, a price list published several times a week by the National Marine Fisheries Service. This publication is not an infallible indicator, because it is several days out of date and because many deals are secret. It does not reflect prices paid in other parts of the region, which differ somewhat from those in Boston. A lot of information is obtained by calling business associates who are at the same level in the marketing chain, but the best indicator of real prices and market activity is provided by the negotiating process itself. Thus, large firms, with representatives constantly on the phone to dealers, pound operators, and marketing firms from Canada to Florida, have an edge in the negotiating process over the small dealer who dickers with only one or two wholesalers. As one co-op manager explained, "When you are dealing with the large Boston wholesalers, you don't dicker much; you either take the price they offer or leave it." The small firms are aware that the big ones have better data and watch them closely. For these smaller operations, the prices set by large, vertically integrated firms substitute for more precise information about supply and demand in the market.

Sometimes an individual wholesaler or dealer suddenly increases the price he pays for lobster, and the change reverberates up and down the coast, establishing a new price. Without question, the most important factor involved in price increases is supply. According to one wholesaler, "the reason the price jumps up is [that] someone got short of lobster and hiked the price to get more." Others in need of lobsters follow suit.

Expectations also play a role. Just after Labor Day, people expect prices to fall sharply, but in the late fall and winter, they know prices will rise. They are always reluctant, however, to be the first to change prices. The first firms to lower the price anger their fishermen; raising prices does not please wholesalers and distributors. It is better to be able to claim that your prices are following a general trend.

The process by which prices are negotiated and changed is deliberately hidden from fishermen. To avoid unwanted competition, dealers or wholesalers are disinclined to give information on markets and sources to anyone, but they are especially reluctant to talk to fishermen. No dealer wants to admit to lowering prices. Dealers have several ways of obscuring the way prices are changed and their own role in the process. They talk about price movements as if magical forces, rather than human decisions, were responsible: "The price is moving up." Price changes are commonly blamed on the largest companies. Bay State Lobster is often forced to play the role of villain. Some dealers and wholesalers play a double-edged game in which they take credit for price rises, which please fishermen, but never take responsibility for price drops. Naturally, many astute fishermen see through this strategy. Gene Witham of Owls Head pointed out that "when dealers raise prices, they are quick to take the credit. When the price gets lowered, it is always someone else far to the westward who did it and they are forced to go along. Somehow you can never find out who the first one was that cut the price."

The subject of marketing elicits vituperation from the mildest of fishermen. In conversations two assertions stand out: (1) the Canadians are allowed to import large amounts of lobster into the United States, which depresses the price of Maine fishermen, and (2) the price of lobster is controlled by a conspiracy in the marketing chain. Evidence does not support either of these beliefs.

Lobster prices would undoubtedly rise if the U.S. government were to prohibit all lobster imports, but no such prohibition will occur in the foreseeable future. Given that Canadian exports will be permitted to continue (as will Maine exports to Montreal and Toronto), arrangements that produce benefits to the fishermen of both nations have been made. The Canadian policy of setting seasons so that a large percentage of their catch occurs in the winter (when catches are low in the United States) smoothes price fluctuations and adds many millions of dollars to the income of lobster fishermen in the United States and in Canada (Contas and Wilson 1982).

There is a good deal of disagreement on the ability of the largest wholesalers to set and change lobster prices. Fishermen believe that the largest firms control price completely, and many competent observers of the industry concur. One National Marine Fisheries Service officer, long acquainted with the lobster industry, says of the wholesalers, "What they decide the price will be, that is what it will be." Several dealers and wholesalers, however, state emphatically that the Boston wholesalers do not control prices. Tim Staples, a buyer for a large Portland wholesale and retail firm, said he has "never called Boston to get the price" in his entire career. (The largest wholesale firms have headquarters in Boston.)

The best evidence is that the large Boston wholesale firms do not have the ability to dictate the price of lobsters, although they may have limited influence on price under certain circumstances. These firms jointly do not control more than an estimated 25 percent of the total market. Jim Wilson, an experienced fisheries economist, said the government could never convict the largest lobster wholesale firm of price fixing. "It would be impossible. There are too many other outlets for lobster," he added (personal communication 1984), referring to the dozens of wholesalers, truckers, cooperatives, and dealers who would rush to fill a market if the price were unusually high or low.

Dealers and wholesalers unquestionably have more information about market and prices than fishermen do; and they undoubtedly use that knowledge in their own interests when they can. However, their ability to cheat fishermen consistently is strictly limited. Angered fishermen can and do switch dealers. They can also form cooperatives that can put dealers out of business.

Why, then, does the rumor persist among fishermen and others that the largest firms control the price? To some extent, the hostility and beliefs about price fixing have nothing to do with the objective facts about the market. The dependence on dealers, who always know so much more than fishermen about the market, brings out the dark side of the Maine character, which sometimes finds its voice in slander. In addition, fishermen are price takers. They have a strong incentive to go fishing when lobsters are plentiful regardless of how frustratingly low prices are. But the whole problem cannot be explained in terms of frustrated behavior and the use of gossip as a means of maintaining equality. Some aspects of the market do lead the fisherman to the conclusion that prices are rigged. His own dealer, he knows, spends hours on the phone talking to other dealers. He is aware that price changes can be started by one dealer or wholesaler, whom people know by name, and that these changes can spread quickly up and down the coast. Moreover, small dealers and wholesalers are only too happy to foster the notion that prices are set by the large companies, in order to obscure their own role in the process. The largest Boston wholesalers are often among the first to make price changes, which helps to perpetuate the myth of their market power. Also, fishermen know that dealers will take advantage of them in negotiations if they can. The highly personal nature of the market adds up to a rigged price in their minds.

None of this, however, signifies an ability to control prices. It is one thing to be first to change prices, to be successful in negotiating and even in deceiving fishermen; it is quite another to be able to set prices in the face of periodic gluts and scarcity. All wholesale firms—even some of moderate size—occasionally see a price they negotiated ripple through the industry, but not one of them controls such a high percentage of the market that it can consistently establish the price of lobsters. The market is reasonably competitive, with price changes that occur because of the well-advertised bidding activities of one or more known firms. Impersonal market forces determine prices, but they need to be activated.

Cooperatives

Cooperatives are a recent phenomenon in the lobstering industry. Three of the seventeen operating in Maine in the 1980s were established in the late 1940s. The most important factor in their formation was conflict between dealers and fishermen. Fishermen, unhappy with the low prices they were receiving, blamed dealer collusion. There are stories of dealers rigging scales, selling illegal or "short lobsters," and using bait supplies to drive hard bargains. Roger Frey, of the University of Maine faculty, whose grandfather fished out of South Bristol in the 1930s and 1940s, recalls that "if you wanted bait, you had to sell to them regardless of the price they were offering." In 1947 Jimmy Brackett and two other World War II veterans started the Pemaquid Harbor Cooperative to break the monopoly of the two area dealers, brothers who consistently paid lower prices for lobsters than dealers in other regions.

The other co-ops were formed in the early 1970s, when fishermen began to take an increasing interest in the idea. The slightest slip on the part of a dealer became a pretext for co-op formation. Not all cooperatives originated in conflict, however. The Swans Island Cooperative was formed in 1973 when the old dealer retired and no one was willing to take his place. The fishermen bought the dealer's dock and equipment and established a cooperative. One manager of a cooperative says, "Fishermen like the idea of cooperatives. They like the idea of running their own business, and not working for someone else. They also like the idea of having a manager who is going to look out for their interest too."

Although it would be difficult to prove, cooperatives almost certainly have helped their members. Cooperative managers pass higher prices on to fishermen and have been very aggressive in raising the boat price. In this respect, they are unlike private dealers, who are indifferent to boat price as long as they can get their fixed markup. Some co-op managers have also been active in searching out markets. At least two cooperatives ship large quantities of lobsters directly to distant distributors, completely bypassing wholesalers in Boston and New York. They also sell large amounts of lobster to individual truckers.

The success of lobster-fishing cooperatives has also helped fishermen who continue to do business with private dealers. The formation of cooperatives has lifted the veil of secrecy from prices and markets. Since it is common knowledge that the cooperative managers try to get as high a price as possible for their members, the cooperative price has become the benchmark used by all fishermen in Maine to assess whether or not they are being treated fairly. As Ed Drisko of New Harbor puts it, "What the co-op has done is give us a window into that crooked marketing system."

There are costs to belonging to cooperatives. Co-op members do not have the opportunity to get loans, special prices, or other favors granted by private dealers. They must attend board meetings, and the officers of the cooperatives are often required to spend considerable amounts of time setting policy, listening to complaints, and so on. There are other costs too. One fisherman said, "Around the co-op now there is a lot of tension. There's a lot of grudges. We have had several meetings with people shouting at each other. Nothin' useful got done."

Nor have the cooperatives turned out to be as profitable as fishermen might have hoped. Many have been plagued by conflict, managerial problems, inefficiency, and low profits. Primary sources of conflict are suspected favoritism on the part of the manager and managerial incompetence. Undoubtedly, co-ops have had a large number of incompetent managers as a result of the practice of hiring young men whose only qualifications were their well-established families and their willingness to work long hours in the office and on the dock. Managerial ability was clearly of secondary concern (Fox and Lesser 1983: 22).

Even when managers are perfectly competent, their decisions come under intense scrutiny, and co-op members or officers are constantly trying to influence their decisions. As one former manager expressed it, "Life for a co-op manager is just sheer hell." In many instances conflicts have reached explosive proportions. One manager from a religious community has a unique way of handling raucous co-op meetings: he prays until the members stop arguing. Another very competent manager periodically resorts to fisticuffs. On one occasion, he threw the president of the cooperative off the dock.

Not surprisingly, turnover among managers is high. Since 1971, the average tenure has been less than two years (Fox and Lesser 1983: 23). In many cases, conflict and lack of profit reinforce each other in a downward spiral. If the profitability of the co-op is low, the fishermen become resentful, and the result is a loss of freedom for the manager and an undermining of his authority. As the level of conflict rises, fishermen are more likely to sell a higher percentage of their catches to private dealers or other markets. Both the restrictions and the loss of volume lead to further loss of revenue and profits. A few cooperatives have been able to avert this downward cycle by appointing competent managers and leaving them free to operate without interference. Usually these managers are older men who have some experience in business and are more likely to gain the respect of fishermen.

If managing one cooperative is difficult, coordinating several has proved impossible. In the late 1970s, the Maine Association of Cooperatives, "Big Mac," was formed to market the catches of member cooperatives in the hope of obtaining very high prices. Big Mac's joint marketing effort failed after a few months, because of severe conflict among member cooperatives. A major problem was that Big Mac hired truck drivers to manage the operation because they supposedly were familiar with the city markets. Competence in finance, marketing, and personnel management were scarcely considered.

Ironically, at present the benefits of cooperatives may accrue much more to the men who still sell to private dealers than to members of the seventeen cooperatives themselves. As noted earlier, the most important benefit to all fishermen is that the strong negotiating position of cooperative managers keeps the boat price of lobsters at higher levels all along the coast.

Cooperatives have also forced private dealers to increase their services to fishermen. After 1975, when it became obvious that cooperatives were succeeding and more were being considered, dealers became especially attentive to their fishermen. Some built freezer plants to ensure a steady, secure supply of bait; others increased their loans to fishermen.

The advantages in belonging to cooperatives seem to be few. Members must endure a lot of conflict and forgo the loans and other "perks" offered by dealers. Under these conditions, one might expect a mass defection from the co-ops, but it is not occurring. Cooperatives now are well established on the Maine coast and appear to be a permanent part of the scene. Despite certain drawbacks, fishermen like the idea of being owners of a cooperative rather than fishing for a dealer. More important, fishermen as a group are very aware that cooperatives have forced concessions from private dealers. If they all went back to selling to individuals, the dealers' negotiating position would be greatly improved and boat prices would fall again. But the irony remains. Cooperatives, which were formed to help their members, may now be doing more to help the fishermen who have refused to join them.

CHAPTER 7

Any Port in a Storm

Most fishermen have traditionally wanted very little government intervention. In recent decades, however, state and federal fisheries
agencies have increased pressure for more stringent regulation of the
lobster fishery. Biologists of the Maine Department of Marine Resources and the National Marine Fisheries Service have long felt
that the lobster fishery was being overexploited to the point where
breeding stock was being damaged and complete stock failure was a
possibility. A wide variety of regulations were proposed in the 1970s
to deal with the problem, but fishermen were quick to condemn
many of them.

A study on fishermen's attitudes toward regulation demonstrated
that fishermen opposed a tax on traps—even though many believed
that too many traps were in the water—feeling that such a tax
would be unfair and ineffective. They condemned a proposed mora-
torium on fishing—with compensation to fishermen in the form of
subsidies—to allow for stock replenishment. Many did not want to
be dependent on the government for their income; others feared the
loss of independence or were infuriated by the thought of accepting
welfare (Acheson 1975b).

Support for proposed biological schemes was split. Seventy-two
percent of fishermen interviewed favored removing the oversize

measure, which would allow them to take lobsters over five inches, primarily because it would open a new fishery and make it possible to land the large lobsters caught offshore in Maine. Only a few lobster fishermen were worried enough about the state of the breeding stock to want to retain the measure. The state and federal fisheries management plan for lobsters advocated raising the legal minimum size to 3½ inches on the carapace. The consensus among the biologists is that the increase would allow many more female lobsters to reach sexual maturity. Fishermen were solidly against such a proposal on economic grounds. Most lobsters taken are just over the current legal size of 3³⁄₁₆ inches; an increase in the measure would make a sizable percentage of the current catch illegal. Fishermen did not want their incomes reduced even if there were long-term benefits for the industry.

Eighty-eight percent favored a limit on traps, however. Fishermen generally recognized that there are too many traps in the water. They felt that to limit traps would not cut the total catch or even the catch of an individual; it would simply take longer to catch the same number of lobsters. Limiting traps would also substantially cut the costs of bait, fuel, and equipment. Since fishermen value equality of opportunity, more than 98 percent thought a trap limit would be "fairer" (Acheson 1975b).

Fishermen generally had mixed reactions about limiting licenses. The idea of limited entry came as no shock or surprise, for the industry has been limiting entry to harbor gangs informally for many decades. Rather, their interest focused on who would be allowed to go fishing and who would not. It quickly became apparent that fishermen wanted to exclude those who had traditionally been excluded and include those who had always been granted admission. They wanted to bar the hated part-timers and recreational fishermen but admit special classes of part-timers, such as their own sons and semiretired fishermen. For this reason, they showed a good deal of interest in the criteria for granting a man a license. When a bill was presented in the legislature in 1975 that would have limited entry and imposed a trap limit, reaction ranged from moderate support to violent opposition. Among those opposed were the fishermen from Vinalhaven, who went so far as to hire a lobbyist. He was able to raise doubt in legislators' minds about the constitutionality of limited-entry legislation, and the bill was defeated. From 1975 to the mid 1980s, no serious attempts were made to limit either traps or entry.

Attitudes toward management have changed considerably since 1975 because of a squeeze on profits in the lobster fisheries. Prices for boats rose dramatically. In 1975, a two- or three-year-old wooden boat might have cost $13,000; in 1986 a comparable boat cost $40,000, a 207 percent increase. A new wooden trap with rope and buoy cost $17.50 in 1977, and about $37.00 in 1987, a 111 percent increase. The price fishermen received for their lobsters also went up, but at a far slower rate. In August 1979, fishermen were receiving $1.60 per pound for soft-shelled lobsters; in August 1986, they received $2.20, a 37 percent increase.

At the same time, the number of lobster fishermen began to increase. Groundfish catches dropped in 1984 and 1985, and a number of men who had switched to groundfish from lobstering in the late 1970s returned to lobstering. A 1985 World Court ruling awarded Canada, not the United States, the North East Peak of Georges Bank, one of the world's richest fishing grounds, where New Englanders had fished for three hundred years. Some of these displaced fishermen also moved into lobstering. Meanwhile, the lobster catch remained relatively constant, with the result that fewer lobsters were available per fisherman. An officer of the Pemaquid co-op said that the cooperative was "buying about the same number of lobsters it has for the past few years, but they are being shared among more fishermen." A good many men tried to compensate for lowered catches by putting out more traps, which only exacerbated the problem of trap congestion and increased the cost of equipment. Many fishermen were convinced that catch per unit of effort declined. Men who reported that they caught an average of three-quarters of a pound daily in the early 1970s said that they were lucky to get the same amount now in traps set two to four days. While such declines may have occurred in certain areas or for certain people, in the state as a whole, catch per unit of effort does not appear to have changed (Thomas et al. 1983).

During the summer of 1986, fishermen were clearly feeling financial pressure. One Pemaquid Harbor fisherman reported that his earnings were no greater than those of five years ago. He and his wife opened a restaurant as a means of increasing their income and as a hedge against further decline in the lobster industry. One Casco Bay fisherman, who refused to increase his number of traps to keep up with the competition, said that he grossed some $60,00 in 1975 and only $28,000 in 1984. He admitted that he was not fishing as hard as he had in the 1970s but pointed out that the decline in his catch was far steeper than the decline in the number of traps pulled.

Fishermen in the summer of 1986 were not optimistic about the future of their industry. In a sample of forty-five fishermen, forty-two said that conditions were worse than they had been five years ago. Many experienced fishermen admitted that they would not like to be starting out in the business in the mid 1980s, for they doubted that young fishermen who had gone into debt to get started could survive economically. One said, "There is no way those kids are going to be able to afford to eat and still be able to pay off those $75,000 loans they have all taken out."

Some very good fishermen were so disgusted with conditions that they left the lobster industry. Bob Green of Orrs Island, a thirty-year veteran who last fished in 1985, explained, "There just aren't the lobsters there used to be. You have to fish a lot more traps to catch the same number. You get all snarled up. You can't fish out there with all that gear." He also complained about the cutthroat attitudes of the new men coming into the industry and their lack of consideration: "It used to be fun to go fishing. It isn't any more." Green's son recently switched from lobstering to working on a swordfishing boat. "I'm relieved he made the switch," Green said.

These problems have produced a marked change in attitudes toward resource management in the lobster industry. Certainly Maine fishermen distrust the government and do not want massive intervention in their affairs. But as economic problems in the industry appear to worsen, there is a growing recognition that something must be done and that only the government can do it. Surprisingly, fishermen are unanimous on many issues. The ambivalence toward government action and the wide range of opinion on most management issues, so marked in the 1970s, no longer existed in the sum-

mer of 1986. Of the forty-five fishermen interviewed, almost all
agreed that there were too many traps in the water and too many
fishermen. Over 90 percent wanted a limit on the number of licenses
and the number of traps. Many volunteered that having one without
the other would be pointless. "It wouldn't do any good," one said, "to
limit the number of men if those remaining could keep on increasing the number of traps they fished." They approved unanimously of
the 1974 law requiring escape vents on traps—a device designed to
retain the legal-sized lobsters and allow the undersized to escape.
With vents, fishermen do not have to handle small lobsters, which
makes it easier to clean out their traps and reduces the number of
times lobsters are handled, thus lowering the rate of mutilation and
mortality.

Even more interesting, there was a marked role reversal in attitudes toward many management issues: fishermen now wanted to
retain some important conservation measures that federal and state
fisheries management officials wanted to abandon. For over a decade, the Lobster Management Council of the Atlantic States Marine Fisheries Commission had advocated a standard set of regulations for all states in which lobsters are caught. The cornerstone of
that system is to raise the legal minimum size to 3½ inches, which
would presumably allow a much higher percentage of females to
reach sexual maturity, increasing the number of eggs in the water
and, within a few years, the number of marketable lobsters. The
council would abolish the 5-inch oversize measure, which in their
view is ineffective. (The idea behind the five-inch measure is that
large lobsters are capable of extruding a lot of eggs.) The plan would
eliminate the notching of egged females, which currently cannot be
taken, on the grounds that cutting notches allows infection to enter
and increases mortality. The plan has recently been taken up by the
New England Regional Council and has become the official federal
lobster management plan.

Fishermen felt ambivalent about these proposals. Overwhelmingly, lobster fishermen interviewed in the summer of 1986 wanted
to retain the oversize measure. Of the forty-five men interviewed,
only one wished to see the rule abolished. Most fishermen reasoned
that abolishing the oversize measure would increase their catches by

only a few dozen lobsters a year, since few big lobsters inhabit inshore waters; retaining the measure probably would help to conserve the resource. However, virtually all of the dealers wanted to
see it abolished. They reasoned that large offshore lobsters were
being caught and landed in New Hampshire. The oversize law was
therefore not protecting the breeding stock and deprived Maine dealers of a sizable supply of lobsters.

All of the fishermen wished to retain the notched-tail law, to protect proven breeding stock. In the view of many this law has been
the backbone of lobster conservation efforts. According to one fisherman, "If you do away with that law, you do away with the industry.
It's that important."

Opinion was split on raising legal measure to 3½ inches. Twenty-
three of the men interviewed approved raising it, eighteen did not.
Even those twenty-three men who approved, however, were not en-
thusiastic. They generally agreed that a raise in the measure would
cut catches, at least in the period when the measure was being raised.
Many men believed that in the long run, an increase would protect
the breeding stock and would result in larger lobsters that could be
sold for higher prices.

In an effort to come to grips with federal fisheries management
plans, Eddie Blackmore, president of the Maine Lobstermen's Association, has proposed an unusual compromise. Even more unusual,
state and federal officials are supporting it. His group would support
the 3½ measure, though he and many fishermen feel it is unneces-
sary, if the federal and state governments would agree to maintain
the 5-inch oversize measure and the notched-tail law. This proposal
would give both sides the kinds of conservation rules they feel are
essential. Blackmore, a very effective spokesman for the industry, is
well on the way toward getting such a compromise solution passed
into law.

The Maine legislature passed a law scheduled to go into effect
January 1, 1988, incorporating all features of this compromise. This
bill calls for increasing the legal minimum size ⅛ inch over a five-
year period in 1⁄32-inch increments. The oversize law would be re-
tained, as would the V-notch law. However, this law will not take
effect unless laws are passed to prevent taking V-notch lobsters in

other New England states. (Other New England states have ostensibly agreed to do this.) Whether this package will go into effect
January 1 as planned remains somewhat questionable. The attorney
general of Maine is legally empowered to nullify the law if other
states do not pass laws prohibiting the taking of lobsters notched by
Maine fishermen. He may very well do exactly that because other
states—especially New Hampshire—appear to have made no obvious progress toward passing such a law.

Implementing such a law has an ironical side. It means that a
group of fishermen will have agreed to have one conservation law
imposed as a means of retaining others. The proposal demonstrates
their concern about the resource and their resolve to help to protect
it. Such a concern is not supposed to be manifested by users of
common-property resources. Where have all the rapists of common-
property resources gone?

The fishermen's determination to keep the oversize and notched-
tail laws has a scientific basis, as evidence increasingly shows that
these laws are far more effective than previously supposed. Robert
Bayer (personal communication 1986) of the University of Maine
has found that 68 percent of all egg-bearing lobsters are notched—
strong evidence that notching breeding females helps to conserve
them (Daniels, Bayer, and Vaitonas 1984: 1).

Recent studies also show that the 5-inch law may be helping to
increase the number of eggs in the water. Very large females not
only have more eggs in proportion to their body size but also have
the capacity to extrude eggs twice from a single mating (Waddy and
Aiken: 1985).

There is a wide difference of opinion on the effectiveness of the
proposal to raise the legal minimum size to 3½ inches. Krouse (1972:
11–12) of the Maine Department of Marine Resources puts in a
nutshell the state and federal case for increasing the legal minimum
measure: "In view of these results of the female maturity investigation, we have concluded that: (1) females seldom mature below
3³⁄₁₆ inches (gauge measure); (2) a few females mature between 3⅛ to
3½ inches (80 to 90 mm); and (3) at sizes larger than 3⅞ inches
(100 mm) nearly all females are mature. Maine's minimum size
limit of 3³⁄₁₆ inches (81 mm) is obviously not allowing most female

lobsters the opportunity of spawning at least once before being har-
vested." Along with the fishermen, biologist Robert Bayer (personal
communication 1987) is more dubious. He argues that recent data
show that such an increase in the measure would raise the number
of egg-bearing females by only 4 percent in Maine. Further south,
where water temperatures are higher, there would be a higher yield
of egg-bearing lobsters from raising the measure.

The biological data alone do not address the issue of most concern
to the fisherman—the way their incomes would be effected by such
an increase. A study that my crew did in the early 1980s shows that
if the minimum legal measure were raised to 3½ inches in ¹⁄₁₆-inch
intervals for five years, there would be a decline in both total catch
and total revenue to Maine fishermen in all five years that the measure was increased. After the legal measure reached 3½ inches, there
would most likely be a 5.5 percent increase in total revenue to Maine
lobster fishermen and a 13 percent return on investment (Acheson
and Reidman 1982a: 9–10). Thus, in the long run, the raise to 3½
inches would benefit the industry economically and increase the
biomass of lobsters. The problem would come in the period when
the law was being implemented in the form of economic hardship
for fishermen.

What of the future? Tourists and casual observers of the Maine
scene view the lobster industry as a rather quaint, perhaps disap-
pearing, holdover from the nineteenth century. My own suspicion is
that the lobster industry will endure, and in much the same form.
Nothing more efficient than the trap has yet been devised to take
lobsters; and regardless of their number, traps certainly are not capable of wiping out the lobster population. Many men might be
forced to leave the industry if stock failure occurred, but substantial
numbers of lobsters would survive. Stock failure is unlikely, the predictions of biologists notwithstanding. In fact, the catch has been remarkably stable since 1947, when consistent catch records began to
be maintained.

The lobster industry is unlikely to succumb to corporate America,
which would make the lobster fisherman nothing more than an employee of a multinational corporation. Several factors inhibit large
firms from buying boats and hiring their own fishermen. It is very

difficult to supervise fishermen at sea. A corporation hiring fishermen to operate boats would almost certainly sustain higher-than-average costs for bait, fuel, maintenance, and trap losses. In addition, the value placed on independence makes fishermen reluctant to seek such employment. Any would-be entrepreneur who attempted to set himself up as a dealer and hire a number of fishermen would be forced to deal with the territorial system, since the primary purpose of the territories is to limit access.

It would be difficult for a large firm to acquire a number of dealerships, wholesale houses, and retail outlets. The three vertically integrated firms apparently have problems of coordination between the central office and the widely scattered pounds, dealerships, and markets. They attempt to solve these problems by becoming silent partners of the men who own the pounds and dealerships rather than making outright purchases. In the early 1970s, a conglomerate explored the possibility of forming a large, vertically integrated combine of dealerships, pounds, and trucking operations. After surveying the problems and possibilities, it decided not to enter the lobster industry. Nothing akin to agribusiness will dominate the lobster industry in the foreseeable future.

If this prediction proves accurate, lobster fishermen will enter the twenty-first century operating their own boats and small firms as they do now, organized in harbor gangs and dealing with a marketing chain that will be relatively unchanged. They will operate in an environment of greater concern for the lobster resource, with more laws promulgated to protect that resource. Until now, fishermen have tried to conserve lobsters by restricting entry into the industry through the territorial system. The next few years may well witness a new direction in their conservation efforts—reliance on governmental authority. If so, fishermen will combine local-level management and what anthropologist Lynn Pinkerton (personal communication 1985) calls a co-management system (with the state of Maine). The case history of the Maine lobster will thus have helped to modify and extend our ideas about the nature of common-property resources, contradicting those who believe that the "tragedy of the commons" (Hardin 1968) can be averted only by draconian and autocratic governmental action.

CHAPTER 8

Theory and Conclusion

This book contributes to five theoretical issues in anthropology and the social sciences.

Common-Property Resources

According to the theory of common-property resources, resources such as fish, air, water, and publicly owned parks and forests are overexploited and abused in ways that privately owned resources are not. Owners of private property protect their resources, while those exploiting publicly owned or open-access resources are locked into a system that makes unlimited exploitation rational. Why should one cattleman, logger, or polluter conserve the resources, since he cannot capture the benefits for himself? Under these circumstances, it is only logical for such a person to expand the amount of capital he uses and strive to use as much of the resources as possible and as fast as possible. The result is what Garrett Hardin (1968: 1245–46) has called the "tragedy of the commons." In the case of fisheries, the "tragedy" is said to result in overexploitation of fish stocks, decline of the breeding stock, "overcapitalization," and "economic inefficiency" (Acheson 1975a: 205). Two different kinds of solutions have been suggested for such common-property problems. Many of the economists who have developed this body of theory see salvation in establishing private property rights of one kind or another. Hardin, a biologist, is more pessimistic. He believes such problems can be solved only by draconian government controls.

Although the theory of common-property resources has played a key role in shaping current conceptions of resource management, little empirical work has been done to verify this theory. The data presented in chapter 4 and the appendix on the biological and economic effects of territoriality substantiate and repudiate different aspects of it. One axiom of the theory is that property rights help to conserve resources, promote economic efficiency, and result in higher incomes. This case study confirms this axiom. In the perimeter-defended areas, where access is more limited and property rights are more vigorously enforced, the stock of lobsters is larger, catches of fishermen are larger, and the breeding stock is larger. However, the theory assumes that there are really only two kinds of ownership: private ownership and having no control over access at all. As Bromley and a number of other authors have recently pointed out, there are really three different kinds of property: private property, communal or jointly owned property, and "open access" (Jarmul 1987: 4–5). Maine lobstering territories are an instance of joint or communal property. Such institutions, which can be generated by local communities operating on their own, can be effective in conserving the resources. This case study reinforces a point made by Ciriacy-Wantrup and Bishop (1975), that the problem is not "common property" but "open access," or no controls at all on usage. It also helps to modify Hardin's theory by pointing out that governmental action and private property are not the only solutions to resource problems. An alternative solution is a communal property arrangement.

Maine lobster territories are not unique in this respect. A large number of local communities have generated a wide variety of institutions to control exploitation of the resources on which their livelihood depends (McCay and Acheson 1987: 10–15). Though tragedies of the commons (more accurately, tragedies of "open access") do exist in both the third world and the developed world, they are not inevitable in the absence of private property (Acheson 1988).

Maine lobstering territories have not been an unqualified success

in conserving the resource. They have limited the numbers of fishermen entering the fishery, but except in those few places where informal or formal trap limits are imposed (e.g., Swans Island), they have
not helped to limit the number of traps and the escalation of fishing
effort.

The Lobster Market: A Relational System

The organization of firms in the Maine lobster industry scarcely fits
the textbook model. Owners of these firms do not act like economic
optimizers, who buy from the lowest-priced source and sell to the
highest bidder. Rather, the industry is characterized by many small
enterprises—fishermen, dealers, wholesalers, truckers—who have
long-standing ties to one another. Fishermen get far more from their
ties with a dealer than boat price alone would indicate. Yet prices
appear to be set by competitive bidding on the whole. Under what
conditions do such marketing arrangements arise? In the past few
years, Coase (1952), Williamson (1975), Macneil (1978), and others
interested in elementary transactions have developed a body of ideas
that shed light on this question.

These economists point out that economic exchanges can be
placed along a continuum. At one end is the classical market, in
which price is the best source of information, exchange does not depend on the ties between buyer and seller, and the relationship between parties to the exchange lasts no longer than the time it takes
to complete the business between them. At the other end are what
Williamson calls "hierarchies"—large organizations composed of
units that exchange between themselves on a permanent basis. Large
vertically integrated firms comprise one common type of hierarchy
(Williamson 1975). In these firms different departments accomplish
specialized tasks coordinated by an owner.

Between the two are what Macneil (1978) calls "relational contracting." In this case, parties to an exchange are different firms, but
transactions between them take place according to complicated for-
mulas, which are generated over long time periods. Both prices and
personal relationships strongly influence exchanges.

The lobster market comes closest to a relational market, although there are strong elements of a classical market as well. The relationship between buyer and seller does matter. At the same time, lobster prices and quantities bought and sold are strongly influenced by supply and demand.

Why have hierarchies (i.e., vertically integrated firms) not come about in the lobster industry? Why has not one firm bought up a large number of boats, dealerships, and pounds and hired fishermen and others to run them? The development of such firms or hierarchies is exactly what one would expect according to Williamson. Hierarchies, he says, come about when "external transactions costs" (i.e., the costs of making exchanges between firms) are high; they are high as the result of opportunism (cheating) and asymmetrically distributed information between parties to an exchange (Williamson 1975: 29–31). Under these circumstances, it is cheaper, or economically rational, to have several different productive processes done by different departments of a single firm under a single owner.

Exactly this situation prevails in the lobster industry. Dealers have much more information than fishermen, and they have not been reluctant to use it to their own best advantage.

Why have vertically integrated firms not come about? The answer is that social and cultural factors would prevent such a firm from being formed. Any entrepreneur who tried to buy several boats and hire men to run them would immediately run afoul of the territorial system and the men who "own" the areas where they sought to fish. The three large Boston-based marketing firms (Hook, Look, and Bay State) have never tried to operate fishing boats. Moreover, managerial problems and distance would plague any person seeking to run multiple pounds and dealerships. Again the lesson of the three large companies is instructive. They avoid these problems by becoming silent partners with private dealers rather than buying many dealerships and hiring labor to manage them. The problems of trying to manage or coordinate several cooperatives or dealerships can be formidable. "Big Mac," which tried to coordinate several cooperatives, failed for exactly these reasons (see chapter 6).

Although there are structural blocks to forming large fishing and marketing firms in the lobstering industry, the advantages of hierarchy remain. As a result, fishermen and dealers form long-standing relationships in which the dealers give a steady market, loans, and supplies at nominal markups. Such deals maintain fishing firms and marketing firms as distinct entities but still provide many of the benefits of a hierarchy. They reduce the problems of obtaining information, which fishermen would face if they tried to market their lobsters to the highest bidder, and also give dealers an incentive to curb their opportunistic behavior. The dealers gain a steady supply of lobsters to supply their customers (Acheson 1985a, 1985b).

The data from the industry suggest that such relational contracts come about in situations in which opportunism and differential access to information make hierarchies highly desirable, but cultural and social factors make them impossible to generate: This conclusion does not really contradict Williamson (personal communication 1984), who considers markets and hierarchies as the extremes on a continuum, with many other kinds of organizational modes falling in between. The kind of long-term dyadic ties characteristic of the Maine lobster market are one type of intermediary organization.

Skill, Information, and Fishing Clusters

Fish are not spread uniformly in the ocean; rather, they are concentrated in certain locations, which change periodically. Humans exploiting the sea have to decide daily where to fish, and their productivity—with all that indicates for business failure or even starvation—depends largely on this decision. The past few years have seen the beginning of a sizable body of literature on fishing strategies and decision making under conditions of extreme uncertainty.

One important argument concerns the existence and importance of fishing skills. Many students of fishing societies have noted the wide difference in catches taken by fishermen in the same fishery. Wadel (1972) says that in Norway some herring boats catch as much as five times more than the average boat. Differential success has been noted in Puerto Rico by Poggie (1979), in Brazil by Cordell (1974), and in the Maine lobster fishery (see chapter 5).

Differences in fishing success are due to many variables, which undoubtedly differ from fishery to fishery. Some of the factors that affect lobster catches—such as trap size, type of heads, and bait—would be irrelevant in a net fishery, for example. While most social scientists and the fishing public at large attribute these differences in catches to fishing skill (Barth 1966; Cordell 1974; Forman 1967; Heath 1976; Norr and Norr 1978; Poggie 1979; Wadel 1972), this point of view is not universal by any means. Durrenberger and Palsson (1983: 323) have labeled this belief in the effectiveness of skill a "myth" and a "false ideology" and have argued that factors such as boat size and effort largely explain variations in catches. Elsewhere they argue that a large part of the variance in Icelandic herring catches is due to the randomness of herring behavior (Palsson and Durrenberger 1983: 516–17). Their work has stirred up considerable debate among maritime anthropologists (Gatewood 1984; McNabb 1985).

Durrenberger and Palsson, to their credit, have gathered a good deal of quantitative data to support their argument. Despite popular belief in the existence of personal fishing skill, very few statistical studies support that view. My own data from the Maine lobster fishery help to fill that gap. Although a large number of factors influence catches, I found solid evidence that one of the key factors explaining the differences in catches is the placement of traps. In this book I have also stressed the detailed information that fishermen must have to place traps properly and have shown how much such skills are worth economically. Another statistical study also reinforced the importance of personal skill (Acheson 1980a, 1980b). While a complete description of this study is beyond the scope of this book, I can summarize the conclusions. After measuring seventeen variables thought to affect catches—including technical, environmental, locational, and personal traits of fishermen—and analyzing them using multiple stepwise regression, I found that skill was undoubtedly one of the most important variables. Only the size of the trap and the season variables had more influence on catches than the skill of the individual fisherman (Acheson 1980b: 28).

A second argument concerns the ways fishermen obtain information. There are two ways a fisherman can obtain data on good fishing locations: from his own knowledge and experience, and from other fishermen, either by direct communication or by direct observation.

Most fishermen do both, which means that fishermen are joined into networks or clusters. It was Barth (1966) who first noted that fishermen in clusters were organized in a prestige hierarchy based on skill and success. He also stressed that a fisherman's dependence on clusters was related to his relative skill.

Barth essentially argues that the decisions skippers make depend in large part on their ability to keep a crew. Barth notes that the first fishing boats to find a concentration have good catches; the last boats catch little or nothing. Moreover, he argues, though a fisherman's optimal strategy is to strike out on his own rather than chase other boats, most boats stay within sight of the cluster and spend most of their time trying to find out what other skippers are doing. Barth's explanation of this unadaptive behavior is that the independent-search strategy demands that the crew trust its own skipper more than the other skippers in the cluster. Since a crew's confidence in the skipper depends on his past success, skippers who have good reputations can thus enjoy more independence than less successful skippers. The results are self-reinforcing. Good skippers can go where they please more often, make greater catches, and gain more confidence from their crews, giving them greater ability to select fishing grounds independently of the cluster.

Other anthropologists have modified these explanations in a number of ways. Gatewood (1984: 351) argues, contrary to Barth, that operating independently does not lead to greater success—at least in the Alaskan salmon industry. He says that sharing information is not additive but "synergistic." Several boats working together can get more fish than can those boats operating independently. Sharing information indiscriminately, however, is not an advisable strategy. Because a fisherman wants to obtain information as valuable as the information he gives, information is carefully managed. In some fisheries, information is given by radio in the clear, but fishermen take great pains to protect essential information until it can be optimally exchanged or can no longer be protected (Andersen 1972: 120ff.). In other fisheries, information is exchanged in secret with only a few other fishermen who can be relied on to reciprocate or because company policy demands such exchanges (Orback 1977: 102; Stuster 1978).

In the Maine lobster industry, information about fishing locations and other matters is carefully guarded. It is exchanged, if at all, only with close relatives, friends, or others of equal skill who can give as much as they get. In this sense, the relationships between lobster clusters are similar to those in other fisheries. There are two important differences, however. First, lobstering clusters are far more territorial-defense units than they are information-sharing networks. In all other fisheries from Norway to Newfoundland and Alaska, no territoriality is in evidence; clusters exist to exchange information. Second, relationships between members of lobstering harbor gangs are far more secretive than is true in other fisheries. One hypothesis to explain the difference relates the amount of secrecy in a harbor gang to the duration of knowledge. If a fisherman discovers a concentration of sedentary species such as lobsters and clams, he can come back and exploit them day after day unless they are discovered by other fishermen. He therefore has a strong incentive to keep such information secret (Wilson and Acheson 1980: 245ff.).

The situation is reversed in the case of highly mobile species. A fisherman has little reason for keeping information about the location of schools secret since those fish do not stay in one place for more than a few hours. Here the problem is to locate concentrations of fish and stay with them. Under these conditions, boats in a fleet actively aid one another in their search for fish. The boats tend to fan out over a wide area and inform at least some other vessels when fish are found. Information exchange is especially marked in cases where a fisherman has discovered a large school: he does not want to leave the school to unload unless another boat stays with the school and can guide him back to the fish for another set (Wilson and Acheson 1980: 252–58).

Knowledge of the Resource and Fisheries Management

Efforts to manage the fisheries resources of the United States have not been an unqualified success by any means. All too often, efforts to regulate fisheries falter because of effective opposition from the fishing industry. Regulations are usually proposed by biologists from federal and state agencies charged with managing the fisheries; their only concern is the resource and the "scientific management" of that resource. Typically, they have little information on the fishermen or the effect that their proposed regulations might have on those in the industry. When regulations framed by biologists are made into law, they can have unintended consequences that result in poor fisheries management (Acheson 1984: 325). Often, attempts at regulation stir up such antagonism in the industry that they find little support in legislative bodies and cannot be enacted into law. This has happened in the Maine lobster industry repeatedly in the past (Acheson 1975b: 662–66). Given their experience, many scientists and managers feel that fishermen have little concern for either the resource base or the future of the fishery (Pringle 1985: 389). Many discount fishermen's suggestions regarding fisheries management on the grounds that fishermen have no scientific background and thus cannot be expected to know much. Others, like Hardin and the common-property theorists, are convinced that fishermen are driven to overexploit the resource.

The case of the Maine lobster fishery may help to modify some of these attitudes on the part of fisheries scientists and administrators. Lobster fishermen know a tremendous amount about the lobster and the factors affecting catches. While that information was not gained through any "scientific" process, it agrees largely with that of lobster biologists. It does not support the notion that fishermen's ideas about regulation stem from what one of my former-colleagues in the National Marine Fisheries Service called "wishful thinking and mythology." Moreover, recent events in the Maine lobster fishery contradict the idea that fishermen do not care about the conservation of the resources on which their livelihood is based. As noted earlier, in the mid 1980s, many fishermen favored more conservation regulations than did federal and state biologists.

I am not suggesting that resource management be placed in the hands of those who exploit these resources. But it is equally naive to think that the social organization and values of fishermen can be ignored. One solution might be to draft regulations that take advantage of existing norms and institutions—or at least avoid conflicting with them. Even better, perhaps a dialogue between fishermen and managers could result in co-management. This has long occurred in the herring industry and now appears to be coming about in the lobster industry as the Maine Lobstermen's Association increasingly negotiates with the Maine Department of Marine Resources, and the New England Regional Council.

Risk, Uncertainty, and Institutions

One of the themes that runs through the literature on fisheries concerns the high risk and uncertainty that fishermen face and the ways in which they attempt to reduce that uncertainty by generating institutions. In speaking of the merchant seaman and fisherman, Fricke (1973: 1) says, "His livelihood depends upon his success in his occupation. He works and lives with others because this reduces the level of risk inherent in working alone." (The idea that institutions can reduce risk and uncertainty goes far back in the social science literature [Commons 1924: 301].)

Much of this volume is devoted to describing the various ways that Maine lobster fishermen accomplish this end. These fishermen use three kinds of institutions to control uncertainty in very different ways.

1. Fishermen cannot control the vagaries of currents, tides, and all the other factors that influence the survival of lobster spat. Through the territorial system, however, they can guarantee that the lobsters in a particular area are reserved for a select group of fishermen. Moreover, the fishermen on perimeter-defended islands help to ensure the survival of the breeding stock and thus the future of the industry in the long run.

2. Lobster prices can change in ways that are not predictable for reasons that are not easy to understand. Fishermen and dealers can use horizontal ties (with people at their own level of the market) to obtain scarce information that is valuable in negotiating prices and agreements, and to protect themselves against unscrupulous trading partners. At the same time, they use long-term bilateral agreements with buyers and sellers to ensure supplies of lobsters and markets,

and in the case of fishermen, to obtain credit, bait (always unpredictable), and supplies at reasonable costs. This marketing system, which has so many relational aspects, is designed not to produce the maximum profits in the short run, but to reduce uncertainty over the long haul.

3. A constant problem for fishermen is how to ensure an ongoing flow of information about good fishing locations in a heterogeneous and ever-changing environment. Fishermen in many parts of the world partially solve this problem by pooling information with others in their fishing cluster (i.e., men using the same gear in the same area to catch the same species). The lobster fishery is no exception. Although lobster fishermen are more secretive than people exploiting more mobile species, much accurate information is exchanged verbally by men at the same level on the skill hierarchy and between kinsmen. Of course everyone gains information by observing other fishermen in the cluster.

These three kinds of institutions do not exhaust the list of arrangements that fishermen in other fisheries and parts of the world use to reduce risk and uncertainty (see Acheson 1981: 277–88), but they are central to the world of Maine lobstering.

Economic and Biological Benefits of Territoriality

To determine the relationship between fishing effort, catches, income, and lobster sizes varied with territoriality, we obtained detailed information from twenty-eight lobster fishermen in six harbors along the central coast in 1973–74: three were nucleated, the other three were perimeter-defended. Two kinds of information were gathered: (1) information on income and (2) information on the size of lobsters caught, the length of the proven breeding stock (i.e., females carrying eggs or with notched tails), as well as the location of traps and number of days the traps had been in the water. Almost ten thousand lobsters were measured with metric calipers during this project.

All data in tables 1, 2, and 3 were gathered during this study.

This study demonstrated that fishermen expend less exploitative effort on the lobster stock in perimeter-defended than in nucleated areas. One reason is that, since it is much more difficult to join gangs fishing perimeter-defended areas, men from those areas have more fishing area per boat than men from nucleated harbor gangs. Table 1 compares the number of boats and square nautical miles per boat for three perimeter-defended areas and three adjacent areas. In all instances, each boat fishing in perimeter-defended areas has more fishing area than those in nucleated areas. But the amount of fishing

TABLE I

Square Miles per Boat in Nucleated and Perimeter-defended Areas[a]

	Harbor	Number of boats	Total area in square nautical miles	Square nautical miles/ boat
Nucleated areas	Port Clyde	39	30.4	0.8
	New Harbor	36	44.7	1.2
	Friendship	95	25.3	0.3
Perimeter- defended areas	Green Island	8	11.0	1.4
	Mctinic (south end only)	7	10.8	1.5
	Monhegan	12	20.0	1.7

[a]Only the boats of full-time fishermen have been counted.

area available to men from nucleated areas is actually far smaller than these figures indicate, because much of the area fished by men from nucleated harbors consists of zones of mixed fishing. The men from Port Clyde, for example, fish some 30.4 square nautical miles, but they share 13.3 square nautical miles of that area with men from other harbors. In contrast, all of the area "owned" by men in the perimeter-defended territories produces lobster at some time in the seasonal cycle, and no part of these territories is fished with men from other harbor gangs.

Perimeter-defended areas have reduced fishing effort by imposing various kinds of conservation measures. The men fishing on Matinicus Island and Green Island, for example, have voluntarily agreed to limit the number of traps they fish. There is unmistakable evidence that a reduction in fishing effort in the perimeter-defended areas has resulted in both economic and biological benefits. In every season the number of lobsters and the average number of pounds caught per trap is larger in the perimeter-defended areas than in the nucleated areas (see table 2). The differences in frequency distributions indicate a much higher percentage of small lobsters caught in the nucleated than in the perimeter-defended areas, and a higher percentage of larger lobsters obtained in the perimeter-defended ter-

TABLE 2
Catch Characteristics by Area and Season

	Season I: August 1 to December 31		Season II: January 1 to April 30		Season III: May 1 to July 31	
	Nucleated	Perimeter- defended	Nucleated	Perimeter- defended	Nucleated	Perimeter- defended
No. lobsters caught	366	767	710	2268	2093	2779
No. lobsters caught per trap hauled	.62	1.29	.47	.95	.70	1.07
Mean pounds of lobster caught per trap hauled	.73	1.64	.565	1.21	.911	1.29
Pounds/lobster	1.16	1.25	1.18	1.32	1.20	1.24

ritories (Acheson 1975a: 199–200). For example, 8 percent of all lobsters caught in nucleated areas were 3¼ inches (83 mm), or hardly legal size, compared with 6.4 percent of the catch in perimeter-defended zones. Additionally, 1.9 percent of the lobsters caught in perimeter-defended areas were 3⅘ inches (98 mm), and only 0.8 percent of those caught in the nucleated areas were this big.

There is also a difference in the gross income of lobstermen from nucleated and perimeter-defended areas. From October 1972 to March 1973, interviews with eight lobstermen from perimeter-defended areas revealed that they earned an average gross income of $22,929 from the lobster industry during the preceding year.[1] The average gross income of fishermen from nucleated areas was $16,499. Despite the small sample, the mean income difference in nucleated and perimeter-defended areas is a surprising $6,480. (The t is 5.54, which is significant at the .01 level.) The primary reason for this difference is that on the average, men from perimeter-defended areas catch more pounds of lobster as well as more pounds of lobster per trap.

However, differential prices play a role as well. Larger lobsters that can be sold as "dinner lobsters" in high-priced restaurants bring a higher price per pound than do the small lobsters; "cull" lobsters bring a still lower price. Dealers are more than happy to buy lobsters from men in perimeter-defended areas who have a higher proportion of larger lobsters to sell. They are also willing to pay for the privilege. It is not uncommon for the men fishing from perimeter-defended areas to negotiate with their dealers for five to ten cents above the going price for *all* the lobsters they catch.

These favorable economic results are undoubtedly due to both the trap limits and the smaller numbers of boats fishing in perimeter-defended areas. Trap limits increase a fisherman's profits by lowering overhead costs. A person with a small number of traps does not spend as much for bait, fuel, and boat depreciation. Trap limits do not reduce catches; a fishermen simply takes a little longer to get the same number of lobsters if he has a smaller number of traps. At the same time, income is higher in perimeter-defended areas be-

1. Net income figures would be more valuable but are almost impossible to accurately compute, since depreciation on boats and equipment is difficult to estimate, and no records are kept on routine maintenance.

cause the catch is shared with fewer fishermen because of the barriers to gaining entry to these harbor gangs.

There is some evidence that the territorial system has favorable biological effects as well. The mean carapace length is smaller in lobsters caught in the nucleated areas (87.8 mm) than in those caught in the perimeter-defended areas (89.9 mm). Thus, more lobsters that have molted into legal size are immediately caught in nucleated areas, and fewer survive to become breeding stock.

This difference in size undoubtedly has a strong influence on the numbers of eggs produced in the two types of areas and even on the long-term prospects for the lobster fishery itself. One researcher has estimated that the probability of a female reaching maturity in the perimeter-defended areas is 1.52, or nearly 50 percent higher than it is in the nucleated areas (Wilson 1975).[2] This conclusion is further supported by our finding that 2.7 percent of the lobsters caught in perimeter-defended areas were egg-bearing females, as opposed to only 1.2 percent in the nucleated areas.

The second biological benefit is that perimeter-defended areas have a higher stock density than do nucleated areas, which means that a larger number of lobsters inhabit a given area of bottom in perimeter-defended areas, with all that that implies for future catches and the vitality of the breeding stock. The standard method of establishing stock density in the lobster fishery is to measure the number of pounds of lobster caught per trap per set-over-day (days the trap has been in the water since being pulled and rebaited).[3] This method takes into account not only the catch, but the working time of the

2. The difference in the mean carapace length of lobsters caught in the nucleated versus the perimeter-defended areas is very small. However, since a very large proportion of females become mature between 90 mm and 100 mm, these differences in size are significant for the fishery since they mean that there is a much higher proportion of mature (potentially egg-producing) females in the perimeter-defended areas.

3. This measure takes into account the number of times the trap is pulled and the working time of the bait. (It cannot be assumed that two areas producing a half-pound of lobster per trap have the same number of lobsters on the bottom, if the traps in one area are pulled more often than those in the other.) The formula for pounds of lobster per trap hauled per set-over-day is as follows:

$$\frac{\text{catch in pounds}}{\text{traps hauled} \times \text{set-over-days}}$$

If a person caught 300 pounds of lobster from 550 traps that had set in the water three days, the figure would be 0.18.

TABLE 3
Pound/Trap Haul in Nucleated and Perimeter-defended Areas

	Season I	Season II	Season III
Nucleated areas	.053 (326)[a]	.11 (313)	.27 (610)
Perimeter-defended areas	.24 (662)	.265 (2245)	.47 (2681)

[a] The first number in each square is pounds/traps hauled/set-over-day; the number in parentheses represents the sample of lobsters in each category. We did not begin to collect data on set-over-days until mid April, so our information on Season I is slight.

bait. Stock densities in all seasons are higher in perimeter-defended areas (see table 3). These favorable biological results are also due to the reduction in number of fishermen and trap limits. Since fewer men fish in a perimeter-defended region, the total lobster mortality is reduced somewhat, although individual catches may be greater. Because fishermen have fewer traps, they keep better track of them, pull them more frequently, and lose fewer to become ghost traps, which can trap lobsters permanently.

If perimeter-defended areas produce both biological and economic benefits, why, one might ask, does the state of Maine fail to institute small areas with limited access? The state and its officers show no interest for two reasons: state officials argue that the administrative and enforcement costs of establishing and maintaining small fishing areas would be prohibitive, and since the whole territorial system is somewhat hidden from official eyes, the beneficial effects of such a system have been only rumors. Fishermen know about the beneficial effects of the territorial system, and in two instances they have been successful in having their territories legalized.

From the early years of this century, Monhegan Island, a perimeter-defended territory, has attempted to conserve the lobster resource in its area by imposing a closed season. The inhabitants of Monhegan persuaded the legislature to pass a law forbidding fishing in Monhegan waters from June 25 to January 1. Thus, Monhegan lobstermen are fishing in midwinter, when the price for lobster is very high and when they have few other economic options. They put their traps "on the bank" in the summer, when they have alternative employment in the tourist industry, leaving the defense of their territory to the state fish wardens. This closed season keeps anyone from setting traps during the critical months of July and August, when fishing for molting lobsters would result in very high mortality.

In the early 1980s the fishermen of Swans Island proposed a bill limiting the number of traps that fishermen can use within the Swans Island area. In October 1984, Maine's commissioner of marine resources, using his administrative powers, agreed to enforce a 500-trap limit within the Swans Island area. The measure benefits the Swans Island fishermen by cutting costs for gas, bait, and traps without sacrificing the competitive edge of skilled fishermen; it also establishes the Swans Island area as a legal entity and charges the state wardens with keeping out "outsiders," on the grounds that they use too many traps.

Notes

INTRODUCTION

1. I have described clusters in the herring industry and the groundfishing industry in Wilson and Acheson (1980: 178–244).

2. A person was classified as a full-time lobster fisherman if he earned over half his income from the lobster fishery.

CHAPTER 2. Kinship and Community

1. Population in these coastal communities has been remarkably stable. Bristol High School class records show that of 697 graduates from 1907 to 1965, a total of 392, or 56 percent, were living within ten miles of Bristol in the 1970s, or had been living in Bristol when they died. This indicates that such towns have a large number of inhabitants from long-established families.

2. This rate of participation is high compared with other places in the English-speaking world. Kurt Mayer (1955: 44) summarized a New York City study of group affiliations, which found that only 32 percent of unskilled workers belonged to any organizations, 67 percent of businessmen, and 98 percent of professionals. Mayer also noted that in Warner's "Yankee City," 32 percent of lower-class people were in associations, 53 percent of middle-class, and 72 percent of upper-class. Schwartzweller, Brown, and Mangalam (1971: 21) report that an Appalachian town they studied had very few secondary groups of any kind, save for the church. Fleming (1979: 24) reports that in the Suffolk (England) village she studied, "villagers generally either do not participate at all in formal organizations, or do so only as pas-

sive members." Strathern (1981) states that people in an Essex (England) village joined very few formal organizations.

3. For a short and well-written explanation, see Robin Fox (1967: 146–47). Kindreds everywhere in the world offer their members a good deal of choice about whom they will "pick" as relatives, whom they will maintain contact with, and whom they will forget. This freedom of choice, however, is not unlimited. In Maine, a person is expected to associate with, recognize, and occasionally help certain close kinsmen. The degree of choice with more distant kinsmen, especially relatives by marriage or beyond second cousin, is much greater.

People begin calculating kinsmen by using themselves as the primary reference point. Typically they are able to recount close relatives and their relationship to them with great accuracy. The farther from ego, the more inexact the calculation of kinsmen. At the periphery, the boundary is not clear. Whom one calculates as kin depends very much on the individual and his memory. As Schneider (1968: 67) said: "One of the first things that anyone who works with American genealogies notices is that the system is quite clear as long as one takes Ego as the point of reference and does not venture far from there. As one goes out from Ego—in any direction—things get more and more fuzzy. This boundary fuzziness or fadeout is seen in a number of different ways. Most fundamental, of course, is the fact that there is no formal, clear, categorical limit to the range of kinsmen."

4. In studying kinship we obtained detailed genealogies on forty-four families. No attempt was made to select a random sample of informants. Some of the information is sensitive. Kinship studies turn up everything from divorces to babies born out of wedlock and first-cousin marriages. Under these conditions, we chose to obtain accurate information from a few people who trusted us, rather than risk inaccurate or selectively edited information from a more scientific sample. We are reasonably certain that the families selected are representative, but we cannot be positive. For every affinal and consanguineal kinsman recalled, we learned where each relative was born, where the spouse(s) was born, the current residence, number and residence of children, occupations, and whether still living—all of this in open-ended interviews. We did not press for information on categories of kinsmen whom our interviewees thought were too unimportant to remember.

5. Despite the importance of kinship ties, people in the coastal communities do not have a very elaborate terminology to distinguish various classes of kin. People refer sometimes to their family of procreation or orientation as "my family" and to more distant kinsmen as "relatives." Sometimes, as Schneider (1968: 30) points out, "family" can refer to all of a person's relatives.

6. The use of kinship ties to obtain tangible assets has been noted by a number of anthropologists. Fortes's concept (1969) of the "family estate" among the Ashante is perhaps the most famous example, but certainly not the only one.

7. The operation of these principles in inheritance rights concerning a

family-owned island and fishing area has been discussed in detail in Acheson and Lazarowitz (1980: 344–51).

8. While we believe such loans are relatively common in small Maine towns, it is difficult to obtain accurate details. "Money deals" are usually kept quiet, but case studies seem to support some generalizations.

9. This typology is my own, not one presented by local people. The terms conform to status differences to which residents of Maine communities respond. Strathern (1981: 24), studying an Essex village, also found it necessary to make distinctions between categories of people not adequately described by local terms. The same must be done in a study of kinship in Maine and probably the United States as a whole.

CHAPTER 3. Harbor Gangs

1. Because this community contains an estimated 750 adult men and only 113 skippers of fishing boats, there is only slight probability that these findings on how lobster fishermen select other lobster fishermen as friends could have occurred by chance.

2. Such tales show the darker side of Maine coastal character and tell far more about the narrator than their intended victims.

CHAPTER 4. Territories

1. This terminology has been adopted from Hockett (1973: 69).

2. "Short-warp" fishing refers to a lobstering technique using traps tied to a short warp line—twelve to fifteen fathoms long.

CHAPTER 5. Tricks of the Trade

1. In 1971, social and economic information was obtained from 126 lobster fishermen living all along the coast. Statistical analysis of these data using both bivariate and multiple regression techniques revealed no overwhelmingly strong relationship between any physical input and lobster catches. When income was run against total investment, the R square was only .39439, indicating that only 39 percent of the variance in income could be explained by knowing that total amount invested. When income was run against the number of days fished, the results were, if anything, worse (R square = .21595). The best results were obtained by running number of trap days against gross income earned. In this case the R square was .55051. These results lend credence to the idea that fishing success is related to hard work and that capital equipment plays an important role (Acheson 1977: 113–114).

The large unexplained variance in both the bivariate and multiple regressions suggests that either a great deal of the variance in income is due to one or more variables not included in the equation or that chance plays a large role in influencing catch. In cases of this kind, economists have come to assume that output is attributable in large part to "skill" (Scherer 1970: 346–47).

2. In discussing skills, fishermen rarely mention business management but rather emphasize technical competence and manual skills. Verbal ability and competence in dealing with people and complex bureaucratic matters, so important in middle-class occupations, are of secondary concern.

3. In this multiple regression analysis, fifty-three variables were used to explain the pounds per trap per layover day of nearly ten thousand traps. Nevertheless, the R square for the last step in the equation is only .14, indicating that all these variables together explain only 14 percent of the total variance in lobster catches recorded. This figure does not mean that the results are false or inadequate, only that a good deal remains to be explained about lobsters, traps, and fishermen. No regression analysis explains 100 percent of the variance, but this R square figure is low. Most of the unexplained variance in catches probably stems from the unpredictable behavior of lobsters. The reasons they crawl into one trap over another are unknown and likely to remain so. James Thomas (personal communication 1979), an experienced marine biologist who spent almost two decades studying lobsters in Maine waters, has noted cases where tagged lobsters are released in the eastern part of Maine only to be caught in waters near the New Hampshire border. Such lobsters passed thousands of traps before they finally crawled into one several hundred miles from where they started. What was it about that one trap, if anything, that distinguished it from all the rest? If lobster behavior is so unpredictable, any analysis of lobster catches is apt to have a very high unexplained variance.

4. To those unfamiliar with the sea, it might seem difficult for a boat to slip away from others and remain hidden on the open ocean. Lobster boats, however, are so small that they are usually difficult to spot with the naked eye from sea level when they are more than two miles away. Even on a good day in summer, haze usually obscures them from as little as a mile and a half away. Sometimes in rough weather, fog, or rain these small boats can be difficult to locate from a few hundred yards away.

5. While the S-shaped curve of innovation does seem to explain the adoption of metal traps, this set of concepts appears to be severely flawed when applied to the adoption of other innovations in other Maine fisheries. See Acheson and Reidman (1982b) for a complete discussion.

6. Fishermen also have had a relatively large number of fishing and nonfishing jobs during their careers. The mean age of the 190 captains of fishing boats in our 1978 sample was 42.1 years when they were interviewed. They had held an average of 1.15 different kinds of nonfishing jobs and 2.55 different kinds of fishing jobs each. It should be noted that these figures reflect the number of different types of jobs held—not the number of employers. If a fisherman worked as a machinist for nine different firms during his career, we said that he had one type of nonfishing job. We were interested in sets of job skills, not the number of job changes.

Glossary

Note: Cost figures are for 1980.

Bottom trawling, or *dragging.* A major technique used in northern New England to catch all species of groundfish (i.e., cod, haddock, hake, pollock, flat fish, and so on). Bottom trawlers operate by dragging a cone-shaped net (otter trawl) through the water, large end first. The mouth of the net, usually 60 to 100 feet wide, is held open by means of heavy "doors" attached to the sides of the net. Bottom trawling can be done only with relatively large boats ranging from 45 to 110 feet long. In 1978, a medium-sized bottom trawler was about 65 feet long and cost about $300,000, new and fully equipped. Dragging is relatively difficult to learn since a man has to learn the tows, or smooth places on the bottom where the net can be used without tearing up, along with learning to use a good deal of electronic gear. A man with five years in lobster fishing needs at least two or three years to learn dragging; some men never learn.

Gillnetting. Gillnetting is generally done in intermediate-sized boats, between 36 and 60 feet long. The average gillnetter is about 42 feet long and costs about $135,000 fully equipped, although many smaller lobster boats are also rigged for gillnetting part of the year. Gillnets are a type of fixed gear. They hang vertically in the water with floats on the top and weights on the bottom. They catch groundfish such as haddock, cod, and pollock, which swim off the bottom, but not true bottom dwellers such as flat fish. Gillnetting is relatively easy to learn. A man with five years in lobstering can put gillnetting gear on his boat and be reasonably successful with six months of experience.

Dredging. Scallops and mussels are caught by dragging a steel dredge along the bottom. The dredge is hauled aboard by steel cable attached to a winch. Dredging is done from boats of various sizes. Many lobstermen rig their boats with boom and winch and go scalloping in the winter inshore with a two-man crew. At the other extreme are boats ranging up to 100 feet long carrying up to thirteen-man crews, which take long trips throughout the Gulf of Maine. Such boats can cost $500,000 or more. These large scallop boats are used for offshore scalloping throughout the year, since scalloping demands permanent changes in the hull (i.e., shucking house), which make it expensive to convert a scallop vessel to any other kind of fishing.

Weirs. Devices used in eastern and central Maine to catch herring. They are constructed out of poles driven into the ocean floor, between which are strung netting or brush to make the walls. Weirs are set in coves and bays known to be frequented by schools of herring. In 1978 it cost about $25,000 to construct a weir. The primary skill in weir fishing is knowing where to build the weir. Once constructed, weirs are relatively easy to learn to use. An experienced lobster fisherman can learn weir fishing in one season—two to six months.

Stop seines. Nets used to trap schools of herring as they enter coves or bays. After the fish have entered, the stop-seine net is drawn across the mouth of the bay, using dories. To enter stop seining, a fisherman needs a net between 50 and 300 fathoms long, "twine dories" to hold the net, and a boat equipped with a hydraulic net hauler. The equipment for an average stop-seine operation might be obtained for about $15,000 to $18,000. Stop seining is a relatively easy technique to learn. A lobsterman with five years of experience can become proficient in two or three months.

Purse seine. A very long, deep net that is set around a school of fish (usually herring) by one or two boats. When the circle is complete, the bottom is drawn up, or "pursed," to close the net. Purse-seine operations often use small planes to aid in locating herring schools. In addition, a good deal of electronic gear is increasingly being used to spot fish. The average purse seiner is perhaps 55 feet long and costs about $300,000 equipped with electronics, net, and seine dory. Purse seining is one of the most difficult techniques to learn. An experienced lobsterman would require at least two or three years to become reasonably proficient.

Pair trawling. A technique used to capture adult herring and other schooling species inshore or offshore by having two large boats tow a big net between them. Since two large boats with a lot of electronic gear (e.g., scanning sonar, loran C plotters, and so on) are involved, pair trawling is one of the most expensive techniques to utilize. One set of Maine pair trawlers is valued at more than $1,500,000 for the two vessels. The technique is also one of the more difficult ones to learn, since a fisherman must coordinate two boats, as well as learn to maneuver a huge net, which sometimes catches up to 200,000 pounds of fish in one tow. A lobsterman would need at least two or three years to become a proficient pair trawler.

Longlines. As the names suggests, long ropes from which baited hooks are suspended. They are used in two distinct fisheries. Small longlines, called tub trawls, are set along the bottom to catch ground-fish. Such lines are only a few hundred feet long and are generally pulled with a small hydraulic winch and baited by hand. Tub trawl-ing is generally done by lobstermen during the spring. Longlines are also used by three large offshore vessels, which dock part of the year in Maine, to catch swordfish far out in the Gulf of Maine. These boats carry crews of five or six men and range from Newfoundland to Florida. Tub trawling is relatively easy to learn and enter. Longlining for swordfish requires at least two years to learn and a boat worth at least $200,000.

Harpoons. Devices used primarily in the summer tuna fishery. Most of the men involved in this fishery go for lobster through most of the year. Thus, it is essentially a small-boat, inshore fishery.

Handlining. In eastern Maine, a number of men catch groundfish from very small boats and skiffs with lines on which a few baited

hooks are attached. A summer fishery engaged in by part-time fishermen, handlining involves only two or three thousand dollars of investment. It is very easily learned as well.

Scottish seines. Very long nets placed in a circle around a promis-
ing piece of groundfish bottom and slowly winched into the boat.
They are an experimental groundfish gear in Maine; only one is in
current use. They necessitate a boat at least 45 feet long and costing
over $120,000 fully equipped.

Herring carriers. Large wooden boats owned by herring processing
firms to bring the herring from seines, weirs, and other devices to
the plant. Some double as purse seiners.

Midwater trawls. Used on very large vessels to catch fish in the
water column. The nets in use are essentially the same as those used
on pair trawlers, save for the fact that they are smaller and towed by
one boat. Midwater trawlers are a minimum of 65 feet long and cost
in excess of $250,000 fully rigged.

References

Acheson, James M.

1972   Territories of the Lobstermen. *Natural History* 81(4): 60–69.

1975a   The Lobster Fiefs: Economic and Ecological Effects of Territoriality in the Maine Lobster Industry. *Human Ecology* 3(3): 183–207.

1975b   Fisheries Management and Social Context: The Case of the Maine Lobster Fishery. *Transactions of the American Fisheries Society* 104(4): 653–68.

1977   Technical Skill and Fishing Success in the Maine Lobster Industry. In *Material Culture: Styles, Organization and Dynamics of Technology,* ed. Heather Lechtman and Robert Merrill. Saint Paul: West Publishing Co., 111–38.

1979   Traditional Inshore Fishing Rights in Maine Lobstering Communities. In *North Atlantic Maritime Cultures,* ed. Raoul Andersen. The Hague: Mouton, 253–76.

1980a   Patterns of Gear Changes in the Northern New England Fishing Industry. In *Essays on Social and Cultural Aspects of New England Fisheries: Implications for Management.* Final Report to the National Science Foundation, University of Rhode Island/University of Maine Study of Social and Cultural Aspects of Fisheries Management in New England under Extended Jurisdiction, NSF Grant No. AER 77-06018, 2: 451–99.

1980b *Factors Influencing Productivity of Metal and Wooden Lobster Traps.* Maine Sea Grant Technical Report no. 63, Orono: University of Maine Sea Grant Office.

1980c Cultural and Technical Factors Influencing Fishing Effectiveness in the Maine Lobster Industry: An Assessment by Fishermen and Biologists. In *Essays on Social and Cultural Aspects of New England Fisheries: Implications for Management,* 2: 644–715. *See* Acheson 1980a.

1981 Anthropology of Fishing. *Annual Review of Anthropology* 10: 275–316.

1982 Metal Traps: A Key Innovation in the Maine Lobster Industry. In *Modernization and Marine Fisheries Policy.* Ann Arbor: Ann Arbor Science, the Butterworth Group, 229–312.

1984 Government Regulation and Exploitive Capacity: The Case of the New England Ground Fishery. *Human Organization* 43(4): 319–29.

1985a The Maine Lobster Market: Between Market and Hierarchy. *Journal of Law, Economics and Organization* 1(2): 385–98.

1985b The Social Organization of the Maine Lobster Market. In *Markets and Marketing.* Monographs in Economic Anthropology no. 4. ed. Stuart Plattner. Lanham, Maryland: University Press of America, 105–30.

1988 Economic Anthropology and the Management of Common Property Resources. In *Economic Anthropology,* ed. Stuart Plattner. Palo Alto: Stanford University Press.

Acheson, James M., Ann W. Acheson, John R. Bort, and Jayne Lello
1980 *The Fishing Ports of Maine and New Hampshire.* Orono: University of Maine Sea Grant Office.

Acheson, James M., and Robert Reidman
1982a Biological and Economic Effects of Increasing the Minimum Legal Size of American Lobster in Maine. *Transactions of the American Fisheries Society* 111(1): 1–12.

1982b Technical Innovation in the New England Fishing Industry: An Examination of the Downs-Mohr Hypothesis. *American Ethnologist* 9(3): 538–58.

Acheson, James M., and Toby Lazarowitz
1980 The Family Estate in Coastal Maine. In *Essays on Social and Cultural Aspects of New England Fisheries: Implications for Management.* Final Report to the National Science Foundation, University of Rhode Island/University of Maine Study of Social and Cultural Aspects of Fisheries

Management in New England under Extended Jurisdiction, NSF Grant No. AER 77-06018, 2: 338–73.

Ackerman, Edward A.
1941   *New England's Fishing Industry.* Chicago: University of Chicago Press.

Anderson, Raoul
1972   Hunt and Deceive: Information Management in Newfoundland Deep Sea Trawler Fishing. In *North Atlantic Fishermen: Anthropological Essays on Modern Fishing*, ed. Raoul Andersen and Cato Wadel. Institute of Social and Economic Research, Memorial University of Newfoundland, Newfoundland Social and Economic Papers no. 5, 120–40. Saint John's.

Apollonio, Spencer
1979   *The Gulf of Maine.* Rockland, Maine: Courier of Maine Books.

Bailey, Frederick G.
1969   *Strategems and Spoils.* New York: Schocken Books.

Barth, Fredrik
1966   *Models of Social Organization.* Royal Anthropological Institute of Great Britain and Ireland, Occasional Paper no. 23. London.

Bennett, John W.
1969   *Northern Plainsmen: Adaptive Strategy and Agrarian Life.* Arlington Heights, Ill.: A.H.M. Publishing Co.

Ciriacy-Wantrup, S. V., and Richard C. Bishop
1975   Common Property as a Concept. *Natural Resources Journal* 15: 713–27.

Coase, R. H.
1952   The Nature of the Firm. In *Readings in Price Theory*, ed. G. J. Stigler and K. E. Boulding. Homewood, Ill.: Richard D. Irwin, Inc.

Cobb, J. Stanley
1971   The Shelter-Related Behavior of the Lobster, *Homarus Americanus. Ecology* 52(1): 108–14.

Comons, J. R.
1924   *The Legal Foundations of Capitalism.* Madison: University of Wisconsin Press.

Contas, John, and James A. Wilson
1982   The Impact of Canadian Seasonal Regulations on Revenues in the Northern Lobster Fishery. Seminar paper, Department of Economics, University of Maine, Orono.

Cooper, Richard A., and Joseph R. Uzmann
 1971   Migration and Growth of Deep-Sea Lobsters. *Science* 171: 288–90.
Cordell, John
 1974   The Lunar-Tide Fishing Cycle in Northeastern Brazil. *Ethnology* 13: 379–92.
Daniels, Peter C., Robert L. Bayer, and Scott Vaitonas
 1984   Preliminary Estimate of Contribution of V-Notched American Lobster (*Homarus Americanus*) to Egg Production along Coastal Maine. Based on Maine Lobstermen's Association V-notched Survey, 1981–84. Draft manuscript, Department of Animal Veterinary Science, University of Maine, Orono.
Dow, Robert L.
 1969   Cyclic and Geographic Trends in Seawater Temperature and Abundance of American Lobster. *Science* 164: 1060–63.
Durrenberger, Paul, and Palsson Gisli
 1983   "Riddles of Herring and Rhetorics of Success." *Journal of Anthropological Research* 39: 323–35.
Fleming, Patricia Harbey
 1979   *Villagers and Strangers: An English Proletarian Village over Four Centuries.* Cambridge, Mass.: Schenkman Publishing Company.
Forman, Shepard
 1967   Cognition and the Catch: The Location of Fishing Spots in a Brazilian Coastal Village. *Ethnology* 6: 417–26.
 1970   *The Raft Fishermen.* Bloomington: Indiana University Press.
Fortes, Meyer
 1969   *Kinship and the Social Order: The Legacy of Louis Henry Morgan.* Chicago: Aldine.
Fox, Catherine, and William Lesser
 1983   *Fish Marketing Cooperatives in Northern New England.* New York Sea Grant Extension Publication, Cornell University. Ithaca.
Fox, Robin
 1967   *Kinship and Marriage.* Baltimore: Penguin Books.
Fricke, Peter
 1973   *Seafarer and Community.* London: Croom-Helm.
Gatewood, John B.
 1984   Is the "Skipper Effect" Really a False Ideology? *American Ethnologist* 11: 350–70.

Goode, George Brown
   1887a   *The Fisheries and Fishery Industries of the United States,*
           Section II. A Geographical Review of the Fisheries Indus-
           tries and Fishing Communities for the Year 1880. Wash-
           ington, D.C.: U.S. Government Printing Office.
   1887b   *The Fisheries and Fishery Industries of the United States,*
           Section V. History of the Methods of the Fisheries. Wash-
           ington, D.C.: U.S. Government Printing Office.
Hardin, Garrett
   1968   The Tragedy of the Commons. *Science* 162: 1243–48.
Heath, Anthony F.
   1976   Decision Making and Transactional Theory. In *Transac-*
          tion and Meaning: Directions in the Anthropology of Ex-
          change and Symbolic Behavior, ed. B. Kapferer. Phila-
          delphia: Institute for the Study of Human Issues, 25–40.
Hockett, Charles F.
   1973   *Man's Place in Nature.* New York: McGraw-Hill.
Jarmul, David
   1987   Common Property Resources in the Developing World.
          National Research Council News Report, March, 2–5.
          Washington, D.C.: National Research Council.
Krouse, Jay S.
   1972   *Size at First Sexual Maturity for Male and Female Lob-*
          sters Found along the Maine Coast. Maine Department of
          Sea and Shore Fisheries, Lobster Information Leaflet no. 2.
   1973   Maturity, Sex Ratio, and Size Competition of the Natural
          Population of American Lobster, *Homarus Americanus,*
          along the Maine Coast. *Fishery Bulletin* 71: 165–73.
Lazarowitz, Toby, and James Acheson
   1980   Pruning the Family Tree. In *Essays on Social and Cultural*
          Aspects of New England Fisheries: Implications for Man-
          agement. Final Report to the National Science Founda-
          tion, University of Rhode Island/University of Maine
          Study of Social and Cultural Aspects of Fisheries Manage-
          ment in New England under Extended Jurisdiction, NSF
          Grant No. AER 77-06018, 2: 295–336.
Lunt, C. Richard
   1975   Lobsterboat Building on the Eastern Coast of Maine: A
          Comparative Study. Ph.D. dissertation, Department of
          Folklore, Indiana University.
McCay, Bonnie, and James M. Acheson, Eds.
   1987   *The Question of the Commons.* Tucson: University of Ar-
          izona Press.

McNabb, Steve.
   1985   A Final Comment on Measurement of the "Skipper Ef-
           fect." *American Ethnologist:* 543–44.
Macneil, Ian
   1978   Contracts: Adjustment of Long-Term Economic Relations
           under Classical, Neoclassic and Relational Contract Law.
           Northwestern University Law Review 72: 854–87.
Mann, K. H., and P. A. Breen
   1972   The Relation between Lobster Abundance, Sea Urchins
           and Kelp Beds. *Journal of the Fisheries Research Board of
           Canada* 29: 603–9.
Martin, Kenneth R., and Nathan R. Lipfert
   1985   *Lobstering and the Maine Coast.* Bath, Maine: Maine
           Maritime Museum.
Mayer, Kurt
   1955   *Class and Society.* New York: Random House.
Norr, James L., and Norr, Kathleen L.
   1978   Work Organization in Modern Fishing. *Human Organiza-
           tion* 37(2): 163–71.
Orbach, Michael
   1977   *Hunters, Seamen and Entrepreneurs: The Tuna Seinermen
           of San Diego.* Berkeley: University of California Press.
Paloheimo, J. E.
   1963   Estimation of Catchabilities and Population Sizes of Lob-
           sters. *Journal of the Fisheries Research Board of Canada*
           20(1): 59–88.
Palsson, Gisli, and Paul Durrenberger
   1983   Icelandic Formen and Skippers: The Evolution of a Folk
           Model. *American Ethnologist* 10(3): 511–28.
Poggie, John Jr.
   1979   Small-Scale Fishermen's Beliefs about Success and Devel-
           opment: A Puerto Rican Case. *Human Organization* 38:
           6–11.
Pringle, J. D.
   1985   The Human Factor in Fishery Resource Management.
           Canadian Journal of Fisheries and Aquatic Sciences 42:
           389–92.
Rogers, Everett, and Floyd Shoemaker
   1971   *Communication of Innovations.* New York: Free Press.
Scherer, F. M.
   1970   *Industrial Market Structure and Economic Performance.*
           Chicago: Rand McNally Co.

Schneider, David M.
  1968   *American Kinship: A Cultural Account.* Englewood Cliffs,
          N.J.: Prentice Hall.
Schwarzweller, Harry K., James S. Brown, and J. J. Mangalam
  1971   *Mountain Families in Transition: A Case Study of Ap-*
          palachian Migration. University Park: Pennsylvania State
          University Press.
Strathern, Marilyn
  1981   *Kinship at the Core: An Anthropology of Elmdon, a Vil-*
          lage in North-West Essex in the 1960's. Cambridge: Cam-
          bridge University Press.
Stuster, Jack
  1978   Where "Mabel" May Mean Seabass. *Natural History* 87(9):
          65–71.
Thomas, James
  1973   *An Analysis of the Commerical Lobster (Homarus Ameri-*
          canus) Fishery along the Coast of Maine, August 1966
          through December 1970. National Oceanic and At-
          mospheric Administration, Technical Report, National
          Marine Fisheries Service. Washington, D.C.
Thomas, J. C., C. C. Burke, G. A. Robinson, and D. B. Parkhurst, Jr.
  1983   *Catch and effort information on the Maine commer-*
          cial lobster (Homarus americanus) fishery, 1967 through
          1981. Lobster Informational Leaflet no. 12, Maine Depart-
          ment of Marine Resources Lobster Research Program.
          Boothbay, Maine.
Townsend, Ralph, and Hugh Briggs, III
  1982   *Maine's Marine Fisheries: Annual Data 1947–1981.*
          Maine–New Hampshire Sea Grant Publication, Univer-
          sity of Maine. Orono.
Waddy, Susan, and D. Aiken
  1985   Proceedings of Lobster Recruitment Workshop. Saint An-
          drews, New Brunswick.
Wadel, Cato
  1972   Capitalization and Ownership: The Persistence of Fisher-
          man Ownership in the Norwegian Herring Fishery. In *The*
          North Atlantic Fishermen: Anthropological Essays on
          Modern Fishing, ed. R. Anderson and C. Wadel. Saint
          John's Newfoundland: Institute of Social and Economic
          Research, 104–10.
Wilder, D. G., and R. C. Murray
  1958   *Do Lobsters Move Offshore and Onshore in the Fall and*

Spring! Fisheries Research Board of Canada, Atlantic Progress Report no. 69, 12–15.

1956   *Movements and Growth of Lobsters in Egmont Bay, P.E.I.* Fisheries Research Board of Canada, Atlantic Progress Report no. 64: 3–9.

Williamson, Oliver E.

1975   *Markets and Hierarchies: Analysis and Antitrust Implications.* New York: Free Press.

Wilson, James A.

1975   The Tragedy of the Commons: A Test. In *Managing the Commons,* ed. J. Baten and G. Hardin. San Francisco: Freeman.

Wilson, James A., and James M. Acheson

1980   *A Model of Adaptive Behavior in the New England Fishing Industry.* Final Report to the National Science Foundation, University of Rhode Island/University of Maine Study of Social and Cultural Aspects of Fisheries Management in New England under Extended Jurisdiction, NSF Grant No. AER 77-06018. Vol. 3.

Index